Supplement to
Pattern Changing for Abused Women
An Educational Program

Marilyn Shear Goodman
Beth Creager Fallon

Interpersonal Violence:
The Practice Series

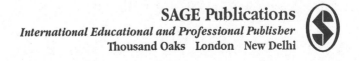
SAGE Publications
International Educational and Professional Publisher
Thousand Oaks   London   New Delhi

For information address:

 SAGE Publications, Inc.
2455 Teller Road
Thousand Oaks, California 91320

SAGE Publications Ltd.
6 Bonhill Street
London EC2A 4PU
United Kingdom

SAGE Publications India Pvt. Ltd.
M-32 Market
Greater Kailash I
New Delhi 110 048 India

Printed in the United States of America

Library of Congress Cataloging-in-Publication Data

Goodman, Marilyn Shear.
    Pattern changing for abused women : an educational program /
authors, Marilyn Shear Goodman, Beth Creager Fallon; with a
foreword by Richard J. Gelles.
        p. cm. — (Interpersonal violence: the practice series ;
vol. 9)
    Includes bibliographical references and index.
    ISBN 0-8039-5493-X. — ISBN 0-8039-5494-8 (pbk.)
    1. Abused women—Rehabilitation. 2. Abused women—Counseling
of. 3. Assertiveness training.   4. Family violence—Prevention.
I. Fallon, Beth Creager. II. Title. III. Series: Interpersonal
violence ; v. 9.
RC569.5.F3G664   1995
616.85'822—dc20   94-31051

> Please address questions regarding any section of
> *Pattern Changing for Abused Women* to Marilyn Goodman.
> Inquiries about available workshops should be addressed to Beth Fallon.
>
> P.O. Box 5646, Wakefield, Rhode Island 02880

95 96 97 98 99 10 9 8 7 6 5 4 3 2 1

Sage Production Editor: Diana E. Axelsen

Contents

1. Your Rights and the Impact of Abuse   **1**
   Basic Rights   1
   Defining the Abuse Problem   3

2. Family Roles and Abuse: Why Is It So Hard to Leave?   **9**
   When There Is Abuse, What Is Whose Problem?   9
   Why It Is So Hard to Leave   10

3. The Dysfunctional Childhood Legacy   **17**
   Factors   17
   Results   17

4. Boundaries and Good-Byes to Old Patterns   **23**
   Boundaries   23
   Old Patterns   27
   How to Change Unhealthy Patterns   27

5. About Feelings: Grief, Fear, and Guilt   **31**
   Sadness and Grief   32
   From Guilt to Responsibility   35

6. More About Feelings: Anger   **39**
   Understanding Anger   39
   Steps for Handling the Anger Within Yourself   40
   Steps Toward Taking Action   41

7. **Boundary Setting Using Assertiveness Skills 1: Myth and Reality**   **45**
     What Is Assertiveness Skills Training?   45
     Definition of Assertiveness   47
     Comparison of Assertive, Nonassertive, and
       Aggressive Behaviors   48
     Women and Assertiveness   48
     Trusting Yourself to Be Assertive   53
     Stumbling Blocks to Assertiveness   53
     Some Myths About Assertiveness   54
     Assertiveness Practice   55

8. **Boundary Setting Using Assertiveness Skills 2: Techniques**   **57**
     Rules for Assertiveness   57
     Assertiveness Techniques   58

9. **Boundary Setting Using Assertiveness Skills 3: Requests and Authority Figures**   **61**
     Why Is Making a Request So Hard?   61
     Why Is Refusing a Request So Hard?   63
     Dealing With Authority Figures   65

10. **Boundary Setting Using Assertiveness Skills 4: Practice**   **67**
     Practicing Assertiveness Skills   67
     Assertiveness and Anger   68
     A Word of Caution   68

11. **Setting Realistic Goals**   **71**
     How to Set Realistic Goals   71
     Achieving Your Goals   71
     I Need . . . , I Want . . . , I Deserve . . .   74

12. **New Patterns of Decision Making**   **77**
     Why Decision Making Is So Difficult   77
     Decision Making in a New Light   77
     Decision-Making Steps   78
     After the Decision   79

13. **Healthy Relationships**   **81**
     Do Healthy Relationships Really Exist?   81
     How Healthy Relationships Begin   81
     How a Healthy Relationship Feels   82
     Problems, Conflicts, and Disagreements   82
     We All Need a Sense of Family   83

Making the Strengths of Strong Families
a Part of Your Life   84

14. Changed Patterns   87
New Understanding   87
Practiced Techniques Form New Patterns   88

Appendix   91
1. Pattern Changing Ground Rules
2. Pattern Changing Registration Form
3. Contract for Pattern Changing Participants
4. Pattern Changing Confidential Information
5. Pattern Changing Progress Questionnaire
6. Your Bill of Rights
7. Outcome Goals for Pattern Changing Participants
8. How Serious Was Your Abuse?
9. Anger Gauge
10. Evaluating Relationships: Healthy or Unhealthy?
11. Recommended Reading List for Participants
12. Pattern Changing Program Evaluation
13. Certificate of Completion of Pattern Changing

1

Your Rights
and the Impact of Abuse

❑ **Basic Rights**

Fundamental to all we teach in Pattern Changing is the belief that we possess certain basic rights in our lives. These rights are not selfish; they belong to everyone, including yourself, your children, and your partner. They are not selfish because they apply to everyone. Your understanding and acceptance of these rights must come first if you want to change the old pattern of abuse and victimization into a new pattern of controlling your own life.

YOUR BILL OF RIGHTS

You have the right to be you.

You have the right to put yourself first.1

You have the right to be safe.

You have the right to love and be loved.

You have the right to be treated with respect.

You have the right to be human—NOT PERFECT.

You have the right to be angry and protest if you are treated unfairly or abusively by anyone.

You have the right to your own privacy.

You have the right to have your own opinions, to express them, and to be taken seriously.

You have the right to earn and control your own money.

You have the right to ask questions about anything that affects your life.

You have the right to make decisions that affect you.

You have the right to grow and change (and that includes changing your mind).

You have the right to say NO.

You have the right to make mistakes.

You have the right NOT to be responsible for other adults' problems.

You have the right not to be liked by everyone.

YOU HAVE THE RIGHT TO CONTROL YOUR OWN LIFE AND TO CHANGE IT IF YOU ARE NOT HAPPY WITH IT AS IT IS.

❑ Defining the Abuse Problem

Among Merriam-Webster's definitions of *abuse* are "improper or excessive use or treatment; . . . language that condemns or vilifies, [usually] unjustly, intemperately, and angrily; physical maltreatment" (1993, p. 5). Abuse is coercive behavior that seeks to **control** and exercise **power** over others. It is a worldwide problem crossing all economic, social, educational, sexual, and ethnic segments of societies. It is found among the rich and the poor, white-collar professionals and unskilled workers, the educated and the illiterate, homosexuals and heterosexuals, and people of all races and religions.

SOCIETAL ABUSE

Societal abuse involves the use of majority male **power** in society to **control** women and minorities. Inadequate legal protection, economic exploitation, and sexual harassment from persons in a position of **power** are examples of this. Signs of progress against societal abuse through the feminist movement are women's right to vote; domestic violence laws, including access to the temporary restraining order (TRO); affirmative action laws; maternity leave; and family planning choices and control of one's own body.

Although we recognize the historical impact on women of living in a violent, male-dominated society, our focus in Pattern Changing is on the victim herself and **her power** to change the course of her life. This focus is essential in helping the woman build the energy and motivation needed if she wishes to confront global problems.

DOMESTIC ABUSE

Domestic abuse is physical, emotional, or sexual abuse taking place within the context of the family household. It may be between adults, between adults and children, or between children. It may be physical, emotional, or sexual. However it may present itself, **abuse is NEVER the fault of the victim. It is 100% the responsibility and choice of the abuser.**

Physical abuse involves the use of any physical act in order to harm, frighten, and gain **control** over another person. It includes not only the obviously severe physical abuse that causes injuries requiring emergency medical care but also any physical contact that aims to frighten and **control:** shoving, pushing her down on a bed, preventing her from moving by holding, and breaking or damaging objects around the victim. It is important to remember that the seriousness of these "lesser" forms of abuse should never be minimized. They, too, are potentially life threatening. A victim is just as dead when she hits her head the wrong way on a doorknob after a "little" push as she is after being kicked down the stairs and stomped to death with the abuser's hiking boots. Physical abuse includes blocking her movements, locking her in a room or out of the house, denying sleep by forcibly keeping her awake, throwing objects at or near her, pushing, hitting, slapping, pulling hair, biting, arm twisting, punching, choking, burning, kicking, throwing her down stairs, and using a weapon against her.

Most abused women say that *emotional abuse* is the cruelest of all forms of abuse and that it hurts far more than physical abuse, leaving deeper wounds that take much longer to heal. Like physical abuse, it is the use of a coercive method to exercise control over another person. It belittles and demeans through continuous verbal manipulation, unpredictable erratic behavior, game playing, and fear, which keep the victim always off balance. In many cases, it is so severe that it amounts to brainwashing. In referring to emotional abuse, we include demeaning the victim, making her believe she is losing her mind and can no longer identify reality, intimidation, isolation, threats, and economic control. Exposed to this abuse for any length of time, a woman or child begins to lose not only self-esteem but also his or her sense of reality. The woman often believes she is insane or sick. The child, though perhaps not the direct target of emotional abuse, is severely affected simply by overhearing it. Where there is physical abuse, emotional abuse is always present.

Merriam-Webster's 1993 dictionary defines *rape* as "an act or instance of robbing or despoiling or carrying away a person by force; sexual intercourse with a woman by a man without her consent and chiefly by force or deception (p. 968). Men and boys, as well as women and girls, may be the victims. *Sexual abuse* is not "just" rape, but includes forcing a person to perform sexual acts **against his or her will,** hurting sexual parts, and treating the victim like a sex object. It is important to remember that rape is rape, even if the victim is married to the abuser. **If a woman says no, then no one has the right to continue sexual advances.** *Child sexual abuse* includes seductive behavior of any kind with a child or young teenager. A child is *never* responsible for his or her sexual abuse, but rather is always the helpless victim of the powerful adult involved. He or she may have confused feelings about hating or enjoying the attention this relationship brought but is **guiltless and never responsible for the actions of the adult. It is entirely the adult's problem and responsibility.**

THE CYCLE OF ABUSE

Most women who are victims of domestic abuse report that the abuse pattern usually occurs as a cycle; this cycle was first identified by Lenore Walker (1979, pp. 55-70). The cycle of abuse contains three phases: tension

Figure 1.1. The Cycle of Abuse
SOURCE: This figure is based on concepts discussed in Walker (1979), pp. 55-70.

rising, the abusive episode, and the honeymoon period. These phases may vary in frequency of occurrence from several times a day to weekly or "just" once in a while, but whatever the frequency, they form a consistently repeating cyclical pattern. Occasionally, a woman will say that it has not applied in her case, but this is very rare.

The *tension rising* phase finds stress between the partners rising to a crescendo until it explodes into an abusive episode, be it physical, emotional, or sexual. Many women report that the tension becomes so unbearable they may do or say something to precipitate the explosion just to end the suspense and terror. It is a time of walking on eggs and waiting in fear for the abusive episode to occur. It may take any form—emotional and verbal, physical, sexual, or a combination of them.

The abuser invariably will blame the victim for provoking the abuse, accusing her of some shortcoming or behavior (e.g., sloppy housekeeping, being too fussy, awful cooking, too fat, too thin, hair too long, hair too short, always late, flirting with other men), real or imagined, that "caused him to react abusively."

Even healthy relationships have periods of disagreement and anger. They are a normal part of living together. If a man is unhappy with his partner, he has a right to say, "I'm angry," or "Let's get some counseling for our problems," or "I want a divorce." **What he NEVER has a right to do is abuse his partner emotionally, physically, or sexually.** It is important to remember that no matter what he does or says, it is the abuser, and he alone, who chooses to be abusive and who is responsible for his own choices and actions.

The so-called *honeymoon period*, which usually follows the abusive episode, frequently finds the abuser apologizing profusely, promising never to do it again, professing his love, crying, bringing the victim flowers, and threatening suicide if she leaves him. This period may be simply an absence of violence and no real remorse. **It may be the most dangerous phase of the cycle because it is during this period that the woman may be lured back into the relationship with new hope, only to find the cycle beginning again.**

❏ **Stressing Positives**

- It is not possible to erase the pain and abuse of the past, but no one needs to be permanently damaged by it.

- People are not identical sample cases in test tubes. As we describe abuse, always be aware that every word may not apply to you. Take what does apply to you, and recognize and respect the uniqueness of each individual and her experience. We can learn a lot from one another.

- When we, as leaders, look at the women in this room, we see STRENGTH, DETERMINATION, and POWER. That is what it takes to survive abuse and have the courage to be here tonight.

❏ **Assignment**

- Ask yourself the following questions: In a normal day, how much time do you give yourself? Who is the central, most important person in your life?

- A gift is something given voluntarily to someone without compensation. It is a present. Give yourself at least one gift this week. It could be a walk in a quiet place, a bubble bath, a 15-minute quiet time without the children, a single rose, watching a television program you choose, or others. The purpose of this exercise is to focus on yourself, your feelings, your needs, and your wants. **In the beginning, you may feel guilty, but it is important to do it anyway!**

- Study Session I text and your handouts.

❏ Note

1. This second right may seem, at first glance, to be selfish. However, it does not mean not considering others or taking the last crust of bread from your children. It does mean that you must love and respect yourself first before you can, with healthy balance, give of yourself to others in the most effective way.

❏ References

Merriam-Webster, Inc. (1993). *Merriam-Webster's collegiate dictionary* (10th ed.). Springfield, MA: Author.
Walker, L. E. (1979). *The battered woman.* New York: Harper & Row.

2

Family Roles and Abuse: Why Is It So Hard to Leave?

❏ **When There Is Abuse, What Is Whose Problem?**

THE ABUSER

Abuse is solely the responsibility and problem of the abuser. It affects the entire family. A man has the right to be angry if his partner does not do her share of household responsibilities, is always late, breaks agreed-on commitments, or is sleeping with every man in the county. **He has the right to complain, to suggest couple counseling, to leave her, or to ask for a divorce. HE NEVER HAS THE RIGHT TO HIT HER, DEMEAN HER, OR ABUSE HER IN ANY FASHION.** Alcohol or other drugs may be involved in the abuse, but they do not cause it. Abusers frequently excuse their abusive behavior by blaming it on "being drunk," "being high," and so forth, but substance abuse merely lowers the inhibitions and gives the abuser permission to abuse. Substance abuse is a totally separate problem and should be dealt with as such. **The abuser's problem stems from his overwhelming need to control and display power,** as well as his inability to deal with frustrations in a mature, healthy fashion, and his unwillingness to grow up and assume responsibility for his own choices and actions. He alone has the power to change this situation by (a) admitting that he has an abuse problem and (b) being willing to seek professional help for his problem. His abuse is learned behavior, and it is his choice and responsibility—and his alone—to decide when he wants to stop his controlling behavior and begin changing.

THE PARTNER/VICTIM

The victim, usually the woman, is powerless to control or change the abuse. She did not cause it and cannot control or cure it. She is not responsible for it. The victim often feels trapped in the seesaw role of being the man's helpless **victim** on the one hand and his **mother** on the other. No matter what form the abuse takes, she and her children live in constant fear of the abuser. She has the additional conflict, however, of wanting to protect and nurture him. The mother/son relationship is one of the principal factors in her reluctance to seek a temporary restraining order, call the police, or sign a complaint. The woman needs to recognize that even though she has no responsibility for the abuse, she herself has a problem if other options are available but she chooses to remain with an abuser who will neither admit he has a problem nor seek help for it. These relationships are hard to leave, and the woman needs much caring support from peers and professionals during this time. **Being a chronic victim is learned behavior and can be unlearned.**

THE CHILDREN

Children in an abusive household are trapped and are as much the victims as their mother, even if they themselves are not being physically abused. Children growing up with and witnessing an abusive father suffer extreme emotional abuse and run a great risk of themselves becoming abused or abusers as adults. They consider violence to be the norm in relationships and in life. Because it is learned behavior, abuse is passed from generation to generation. It would be nice indeed if a child could live with both mother and father, but it is preferable for the child not to have a father in the house than to live with the constant tension, fear, and insecurity created by a frightening, immature, and abusive person. The abuser presents a childish, rather than a fatherly, model. A woman has the right to remain in or return to an abusive situation, but it is important that she be aware of the effects on her children of living with an abuser.

❏ **Why It Is So Hard to Leave**

FEARS AND HOW TO FACE THEM

Fear That the Abuse Will Worsen

When a woman contemplates leaving an abuser, the fears are overwhelming. Most of them are realistic. Despite the horror of living with an abuser, actually closing the door on the relationship is terrifying for most women. If your abuse has been physical, the real fear is of the abuser's finding you and retaliating even more violently than in the past. He may have threatened to take your children or hurt your family or friends. **The priority is for you and your children to be safe.** You may want to spend some time in a shelter for abused women and to seek a temporary restraining order (TRO) from the court. Even if you can afford to stay in a motel, it is usually preferable to go to a shelter specifically for battered women. The isolation, guilt, and grief that abused women usually feel when they leave the abuser can best be helped in an atmosphere of understanding, acceptance, and support from other abused women and from *knowledgeable professionals.*

Fear of Losing the Provider and Not Being Able to Make It Alone

The fear of not being able to make it alone is a realistic one. In today's economy, leaving an abuser who has been a good financial provider and with whom a woman and her children have a comfortable home is a step reluctantly taken, particularly if the abuse has never been physical. The loss of a provider cannot be taken lightly, and being a single parent is a challenge. The question comes down to your willingness to risk staying with a man whose presence is a constant threat to you and your children's emotional and physical well-being. Each woman must objectively decide for herself when the cost of staying becomes too high.

Fear of Legal Processes

If leaving the abuser will involve going to court, fear of lawyers, judges, and particularly the family court process is terrifying for an abused woman to contemplate. Keep in mind that thousands of abused women enter that mysterious and intimidating world every year and emerge successfully on the other side. It is realistic, however, to be concerned about the court system and to cover as many bases as possible before taking legal action; it can be a long process, sometimes lasting two or three years.

Whether or not you like to face it, going to court is going to war. At stake may be the safety, custody, and support of your children, as well as your own safety. Any property and other assets acquired during the marriage will be at stake, as well as possible support for you, depending on your individual situation. This is a particularly important time for a woman to reach out and seek every available avenue for correct information and support from professionals. The most important figure in the process is your attorney. **The first priority is to choose an attorney who knows how to fight and who has some**

understanding of the abuse issue. It is very pleasant if he or she also possesses a sensitive personality, but remember that **you are hiring a person to win in court,** not a counselor, and that is where you need to focus. Although the lawyer's role is not to be a support person, you should **expect to be treated with courtesy and respect.** Obtain lawyer referrals from agencies that work with battered women, and interview each attorney until you are satisfied that you have found the right person for you.

Fear of Loneliness and the Unknown

The fear of loneliness and the unknown looms for many women as the greatest stumbling block in their contemplating leaving. The known and familiar, even if it is abusive, may be less terrifying than the unknown and the loss of a partner. Some women, after leaving, share the relief that comes from being alone and free of the constant fear and control they suffered. Others, however, say it is the hardest thing they have to deal with. They find their greatest comfort in friends and professionals who show support by understanding and sharing of their own experiences.

GUILT

Guilt holds many abused women in a relationship. Most often it stems from the abuser's constant brainwashing that you are crazy, sick, too fat, too thin, a rotten housekeeper, too compulsively clean, and so forth. Hearing it said many times that, "If you weren't so . . . ," "If you didn't do . . . , I wouldn't have had to hit you," takes its toll on self-esteem and the ability to see reality. It becomes easy to assume blame for the abuse and to feel guilty. Guilt also easily rears its head during the tension rising phase of the abuse cycle (Walker, 1979). If the victim has found the tension of anticipating the abusive incident so unbearable that she cannot survive it any longer, she may say something to precipitate it and get the pain over with. She then may assume the burden of guilt for at least partially "causing" the abuse. When you understand the abuse cycle, you will recognize that simply setting off the abuser did not cause the incident. Once the tension begins to rise, the victim can never avoid or stop it. Often the best she can do is to get it over with and hope to be alive by the end.

An additional and significant source of guilt in abused women is what they perceive as their breaking of the marriage covenant. It may be helpful for you to remember that the covenant already was broken by the abuser, who pledged to love, honor, and cherish his wife; he made the choice instead to abuse her.

If your religion is one that believes adultery is the only grounds for divorce, it is hard not to feel great conflict, pain, and guilt if you choose to proceed with divorce because of abuse. Some women at this point decide to leave their churches. Others opt to discard what they can no longer believe and continue to accept what remains for them true and meaningful.

THE MOTHER/SON RELATIONSHIP

On leaving an abuser, even after extreme physical violence, many women express anxiety and concern about whether the abuser has enough to eat, where he will stay, and how helpless and lonely he may be without her. These are appropriate feelings regarding a child, but they are not appropriate to feel toward an adult man. If the victim is in touch with her abuser at this vulnerable time, she will be greatly at risk of being unable to resist his tears and entreaties to return. The reality is that **the abuser is not a child. He is a grown man,** and growing up means assuming responsibility and being accountable for one's choices and actions. **You are not his mother and not his counselor,** and it is time to face reality and let go. To stay in touch with the reality of your abuser's actions, it can be helpful to list the cruel, abusive things he has said or done and compare this with your list of lovable, thoughtful, caring qualities that he demonstrates.

PARALYSIS

When a woman is abused emotionally, physically, or sexually over a period of time, she may begin to feel so depressed that she is unable to make even small daily decisions, and large ones seem impossible. Outside support at this time is vital in helping her take the first steps. If depression persists, professional help should be sought.

HOPE

Abused women tend to remain with an abuser because their hope springs eternal that somehow, if they love enough, their abusive partners will change. Most cling to the fantasy that the dream family they never had and always longed for will somehow work out. A woman may struggle for years against facing the reality of the abusive relationship and giving up her fantasy. This strength in sustaining hope is precious and not to be rejected, but it needs to be brought into balance and channeled into healthy goals that are based on reality.

GRIEF

Contemplating the pain she will feel at leaving a relationship in which she has invested so much energy, time, and love causes many women to put off taking that step. When a woman finally is able to leave her abuser and firmly close the door on the relationship, it is not unlike a death for her and is, in fact, more painful than death, because there is no closure. In this time of grieving, a woman may expect to feel as if she is on a roller coaster ride. Do not be surprised if you feel like crying a lot. The death of the relationship is terribly sad, and crying is appropriate. It helps to know that just being aware of the appropriateness of grief is the beginning of dealing with it.

ADDICTION/LOVE

We often hear an abused woman say, "I must be sick or crazy. I know he's hurting me and my children. The kids are so scared and always begging me to leave. I just don't understand why I can't do it. I guess I still love him and keep hoping he'll change." They report that the abuser's words echo constantly in their ears: "I don't have any problems, and I'm not going to get help. You're crazy and ought to see a psychiatrist, and that's what causes all the trouble. If you weren't so crazy, I wouldn't have hit you. If you ever try to leave me, I'll get the kids, because no judge would ever let a crazy woman have them!" Listening daily to this abusive brainwashing can leave a woman doubting her own sanity, terrified that the abuser is right, and unable to see reality. **The reality is that the abuser, and he alone, is responsible for the abuse! Being involved with him does not mean she is "crazy." It may mean that she has a type of addiction to a person.** The idea that this may be an addiction rather than love usually brings a great sense of relief.

One may define *addiction* as a compulsive physiological or psychological need to surrender oneself to a substance, behavior, or person, even when he or she is aware that it is harmful and self-destructive. Some manifestations of addiction are compulsivity, loss of control over one's own behavior, inability to leave the situation despite damage and danger to oneself and one's children, and denial of the existence and severity of the problem. The presence of any or all of these factors makes leaving the abuser particularly difficult. Most of the women we talk with find the word *addiction* so much less frightening than the word *crazy*. Addictions to food, exercise, gambling, alcohol, and other substances are commonplace in our society and for some reason seem less threatening than the idea of "mental illness." Addictions are very treatable, and, if this word fits your situation, it gives you clues about how to handle it. If you believe you have an addiction to your abuser, just as with alcohol, you need to understand the problem and how destructive it is in your life, be absolutely committed to staying away from it, and seek strong support in the struggle. If you are an alcoholic, you are not going to choose to live over a liquor store and work as a bartender. If you believe you are addicted to your abusive partner, you are not going to live with or near him if you can help it, and you are not going to go where you know he is.

Sometimes abused women also think they are addicted to the excitement and the adrenalin flow that are such a part of abusive relationships. They may believe that they are attracted only to "naughty boys." If a woman grew up in an abusive home and/or with substance-abusing parents, daily life was always insecure and full of excitement and potential danger. Sometimes women from dysfunctional childhoods may find mature, nonabusive relationships boring and too bland. Recognizing this is the first step in working through this problem and moving on to healthy relationships.

❑ **Stressing Positives**

- **It does not help to look back with regret and guilt at oneself, relationships, children, or decisions. You did the best you could at the time.**

- **Understanding what is happening is the first step in changing your situation.**

- **The greatest gift a mother can give her children who grew up or are growing up with abuse is to set an example of seizing control of her life now and thus help them recognize the realities of the abuse. Her choosing another path lights the way for them.**

- **If you have left an abuser, let yourself grieve. This is the death of a relationship. It is a very sad time, and indeed a time for crying. Do not be surprised if the grief comes in waves. Be prepared for the hurt, and know that it will lessen in time.**

- **If you think you are addicted to the abuser, know that it is learned behavior and can be unlearned.**

- **Steps to feeling empowered:**

    - **Recognize the basic rights of every human being.**

    - **Love yourself enough to feel worthy of having them.**

    - **Be realistic about how much your abuse hurt.**

    - **Keep looking at "How Serious Was Your Abuse?" (Shupe & Stacey, 1983, pp. 221-222).**

– Make a list, and put it where you can see it, of all the hurtful things your abuser did or said. Make a second list of things about him that were lovable, and compare.

- **Be realistic about forgiveness. Remember that forgiving the offender may be psychologically possible only when the offender has confessed his sin, repented, changed his ways, made amends to his victim, and begged for forgiveness. In cases of abuse, this can only happen over a long period of time—usually at least a year. It is appropriate, when leaving an abuser, to put forgiveness on hold and consider it, if ever, only after you feel good about and can forgive yourself. It is difficult to view all of this objectively while you are in the midst of the pain. Only time will permit you to see it all clearly. Give yourself this precious time. You deserve it.**

❏ Assignment

- Give yourself a gift.
- Study Session II text and your handouts.

❏ References

Shupe, A., & Stacey, W. (1983). *The family secret.* Boston: Beacon Press.
Walker, L. E. (1979). *The battered woman.* New York: Harper & Row.

3

The Dysfunctional Childhood Legacy

❑ Factors

Although many factors may be involved in a dysfunctional family (see Table 3.1), the ones we see as significant for women in this program are primarily abuse and substance addiction. Abuse may be physical, emotional, or sexual. The victim may be a child or the mother, or all members of the family may share in the victimization. We do know that if anyone is being abused in any way, all members of the family are affected by it. Although we do not believe it causes abuse, addiction to alcohol or other substances plays a large role in a majority of families where abuse is present.

❑ Results

A girl growing up with any or all of these factors tends to become a woman whose antennae are hypervigilant to messages from others, particularly the abuser or addicted adults in the family. She spends her life walking on eggs, focused on listening for the step of the abuser and trying to sense his mood and whether he is dangerous at this moment. Should she try to placate him

Table 3.1 Family Profiles

Dysfunctional	Functional
– Don't feel! Out of touch with most feelings	+ Sensitivity to feelings in self and others
– Lack of honest communication with self and others	+ Honest, open talk
– Child's well-being rarely considered	+ Child's well-being promoted
– Treatment of child by parents is rarely consistent.	+ Treatment of child by parents is relatively consistent.
– Behavior of parents is rarely predictable. The only thing that is usually predictable is that the parents will be *un*predictable.	+ Behavior of parents is somewhat predictable.
– The household is often chaotic.	+ The household is only occasionally chaotic.
– Children often are forced into a parenting role while still very small because parents are physically and emotionally unavailable or extremely needy. Children are cheated out of childhood.	+ Children are children. Parents are parents.
– Unrealistic, inflexible, cruel rules often govern the household.	+ Realistic, flexible, humane rules govern the household.
– **There is a lack of boundaries.**	+ **Boundaries are well developed.**

or simply become as invisible as possible? If she is being severely abused or witnessing it, she may dissociate. These techniques permit the child to survive.

OUT OF TOUCH WITH FEELINGS

The cost of being so finely tuned in to others in the family is, sadly, the loss of being in touch with many of her own feelings. No one has taught the child that feelings are natural and that there are acceptable ways to express them. Her anger is especially terrifying to face, so it is buried and turned inward on herself. She often may feel guilty, ashamed, frightened, invisible, out of control, responsible, incapable, trapped, lacking intimacy and identity, and depressed.

DENIAL AND LACK OF HONESTY AND TRUST

Denial and lack of honest communication are integral parts of dysfunctional families. The child is never taught to seek reality objectively and to communicate honestly with others or, more important, with herself. The entire family suffers from lack of trust. A child growing up abused herself or conscious of ongoing abuse of her mother or siblings can scarcely be expected to have trust. In her experience, some adults are the abusers and others cannot or will not protect her. In cases of sexual abuse, the abuse often is compounded by the caretaking adult's disbelief or blame of the child. Whom should she trust and why?

NEED TO BE IN CONTROL

Because life for this child is totally out of control and she feels helpless and trapped, which she is, she has a desperate and understandable need as an adult to feel in total control of herself, of other people, and of situations that touch her. Frequently, this sense of perceived control, particularly with others, is manifested in her belief that she has the power and capability, through her love and commitment, to solve a partner's problems and change him into the man of her dreams.

LACK OF BOUNDARIES

In all of these dysfunctional families, boundaries are unclear or nonexistent. A little girl growing up in this way often assumes the role of nurturing caretaker of the family. Her sense of identity rests on being needed, and it is not difficult to see how vulnerable these patterns make her as an adult to needy persons, including abusive and/or substance-addicted men.

ALL-OR-NONE THINKING AND LOW SELF-ESTEEM

An all-or-none, dichotomous view of life is yet another result of growing up in a dysfunctional family (Gravitz & Bowden, 1985). The adult woman tends to think that she must be perfect or else she is a total failure. She is either accepted unconditionally or rejected totally. Her demands on herself are unrealistic, unattainable, and exhausting. Life becomes a treadmill of struggling to achieve the unachievable and always falling short of the mark. Low self-esteem is a constant companion.

ADDICTION TO PERSONS

> An addiction exists when a person's attachment to a sensation, an object, or another person is such as to lessen his appreciation of and ability to deal with other things in his environment, or in himself, so that he has become increasingly dependent on that experience as his only source of gratification. (Peele, with Brodsky, 1976, p. 61)

Without the ability to be in touch with feelings and enjoy honest communication, there can be no trust. Without trust, one cannot achieve intimacy. In her frantic search for it, a woman often becomes easy prey to addiction to alcohol, other drugs, food, gambling, excitement, or persons.

❏ **Stressing Positives**

- **Abuse and victimization are learned behavior, and they can be unlearned.**

- **Recognition of negative patterns past and present is the first step in changing them. If addiction is one of them, it is very changeable.**

- **If your childhood household was dysfunctional, it was because of your parents' problems and theirs alone, just as your adult abuse is your partner's responsibility. Your childhood pain did not occur because of who you were or because you were there. You could have done NOTHING to cause, control, or cure the childhood situation. Children are trapped, totally helpless, and GUILTLESS. YOU ARE NO LONGER A TRAPPED CHILD.**

- Most abused women who are mothers, as they emerge from the abuse, feel sad and guilty that their children had to suffer, and they blame themselves. Remember that YOU LOVE YOUR CHILDREN, AND YOU DID THE VERY BEST YOU POSSIBLY COULD FOR THEM AT THE TIME. Consider the period in which you lived and how trapped you felt. No matter how much you love your children, you do not have the power to control or change the abuser. The most precious gift you can give to them is to change your own patterns and begin to break the generational cycle.

- It is appropriate to grieve for what has been lost. Do not be surprised if you sometimes feel as if you are on an emotional roller coaster.

- BEGIN TO FORGIVE YOURSELF!

- The past is past. TODAY YOU ARE A UNIQUE, INTELLIGENT, CAPABLE, STRONG ADULT. Your courageous decision to be here shows your serious commitment to change and growth.

- If you believe, in learning about dysfunctional families, that you are losing all of your identity and are wondering now who you are, DON'T PANIC! You are not losing identity; the many layers of negative learning are beginning to peel off, and real identity is emerging. Try to relax, do not force change, and JUST LET IT HAPPEN.

❑ Assignment

- Give yourself at least one gift this week.
- Study Session III text and your handouts.
- Questions to think about:

  – In what ways do I want to change and grow?

  – Are the people around me supportive of my change and growth?

  – Is my environment safe and nurturing for me?

  – If the answers to the last two are no, what small beginning steps can I take to start to change my situation?

❏ References

Gravitz, H. L., & Bowden, J. D. (1985). *Recovery: A guide for adult children of alcoholics.* New York: Simon & Schuster.

Peele, S., with Brodsky, A. (1976). *Love and addiction.* New York: New American Library.

4

Boundaries and Good-Byes to Old Patterns

❏ **Boundaries**

DEFINITION

Boundaries are limits drawn by each of us that define our separateness, uniqueness, and basic rights. They should not be overstepped. Each individual human being is unique and precious, possessed of a core self that deserves to be separate, sovereign, and independent from anyone else. It is a private core of dignity, self-respect, and a sense of one's own worth and identity (see Figure 4.1). It belongs only to oneself. From her understanding of rights, each woman develops her own boundaries around this private territory. **Boundaries are not a wall against the world; they are an open door for loving yourself and for healthy relationships.**

Understanding and developing your boundaries is one of the first steps toward freeing yourself from abuse of any kind, as well as increasing your self-esteem. It must be done before you can build assertiveness or fully understand the issues of personal rights and responsibilities. **Lack of boundaries is a prerequisite for abuse. Anyone may be abused once, but if your boundaries are clearly in place, you will never be a chronic victim.**

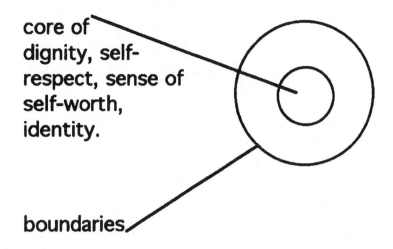

Figure 4.1. Healthy Core and Boundaries

In a functional family, the tiny child, who has felt almost like a physical part of the mother, begins, at about age two, to develop a sense of being a separate, independent person. As the child is encouraged by her parents, self-reliance and self-respect gradually grow. Self-confidence, security, and decision-making abilities blossom as the parents' respect for the child's privacy and boundaries increases appropriately. Parents who have their own boundaries well established teach this best by being role models.

A woman may have developed boundaries as a child but, through personal and societal abuse as an adult, has seen her sense of self-worth, rights, and boundaries gradually eroded. In working to reestablish them, she has an advantage in that she can remember how it felt.

In a dysfunctional family, the parents themselves fail to have well-established boundaries of their own and, because of their own needs, tend to invade the child's territory and/or encourage the child to enter theirs in inappropriate ways. Independence and privacy often are discouraged. Usually, the entire family, along with friends and acquaintances, form a chaotic maze of invasive relationships having no boundaries and forming a tangled web of emotional paralysis.

Figure 4.2 shows how relationships with an unhealthy lack of boundaries can look. You in the center have absolutely no space of your own, and your life is chaotic, exhausting, and paralyzing. You have no developed inner core of dignity, self-respect, self-worth, and identity. The perforated circle represents your openness and vulnerability to abuse that is present when boundaries are not firmly in place around a solid core.

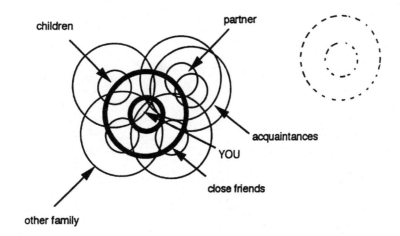

Figure 4.2. Unhealthy Lack of Boundaries

The good news is that Figure 4.2 can be changed into Figure 4.3. Lack of boundaries can be replaced by healthy boundaries, with their accompanying feelings of space, independence, and comfortable involvement with others whose boundaries you are careful to respect. What you may not have learned from your parents, or may somehow have lost over the years, you indeed can develop as an adult. Committing to Pattern Changing is the beginning.

STEPS FOR DEVELOPING BOUNDARIES

1. Understand your rights.

2. With small, daily steps, work to love and appreciate yourself.

3. Give yourself gifts.

4. Be in touch with your own feelings and needs. Needs may be basic and nonnegotiable, such as food, shelter, clothing, and medical care. They may be less basic but of primary importance to you, such as living near your family, going back to school, having a room of your own, and keeping your child in a particular school.

5. Decide, on the basis of your own rights and needs, where you want to set your boundaries.

6. Develop assertiveness techniques to permit you to maintain your boundaries and ask for what is rightfully yours.

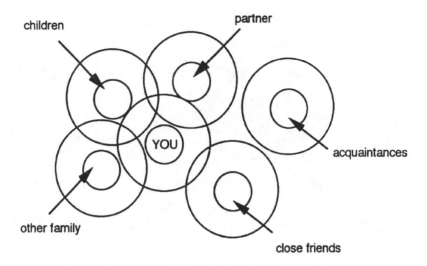

Figure 4.3. Healthy Boundaries

Steps 1 through 4 are concerned specifically with developing one's core of dignity, self-respect, self-worth, and a sense of identity. Steps 5 and 6 permit the gradual drawing of boundaries around the core.

One cannot ignore that establishing boundaries around your core sense of self is not a miraculous protection against all invasive situations. For example, you may have a job you love and are dependent on your good salary. The new boss turns out to be a tyrannical, controlling, mean-spirited person who takes advantage of you, is unappreciative of your talents, and regularly invades your boundaries. You have looked, unsuccessfully, for a new job, and you have tried to talk to your boss to achieve better mutual understanding, but it has been of no avail. Another example is of going to court for your divorce and child custody and having the judge, who is notoriously antiwoman, rudely make every step of the way a frightening and agonizing struggle for you.

These are two extreme, but not uncommon, situations in which your boundaries clearly are being invaded. The price for asserting them, however, would be more than you would want to pay. In cases like these, it is important to remember that you must pick your battles because you can't win them all. It is not a fair world, and there are simply times when a person must live with this sort of injustice and find ways to survive. Counseling and support groups can be a great help in maintaining a healthy perspective as you live through these painful times.

❏ **Old Patterns**

CONTROL

Two things are involved as we work our way out of the control issue: (a) a clear understanding of what we perceive we can control, as opposed to what we really can control, and (b) recognition of what we have and do not have a right to control. We often think we can change other people, particularly those we love, and can work out problems that are the responsibility of others. We think we can guide them to make the "best" decisions for their own good. This is true while our children are very small, but it ceases to be true as they mature. As we understand the rights of all people and recognize and respect our own and others' boundaries, we can begin to know that **the only real control we have a right to exert is over ourselves**—our goals, our choices, our decisions, our responsibilities, our actions, our reactions, and our thoughts.

ALL-OR-NONE FUNCTIONING

All-or-none functioning, the black-or-white view of life referred to in Session III, is a habit of reacting to an outside stimulus in an extreme way (Gravitz & Bowden, 1985, pp. 49-50). It seems to emanate from the lack of development of the inner core referred to in the beginning of this session, and results in little or no trust in ourselves or others, small understanding of basic rights, and low self-esteem. It is exhausting and leaves a woman always demanding unachievable perfection of herself and others and having little balance or common sense. It reflects a lack of recognition of your own and others' rights. Awareness of this habit is the first step in changing it.

❏ **How to Change Unhealthy Patterns**

1. Identify the patterns you want to change.

2. Be aware of the negative habits that form the framework of this old pattern (see Table 4.1).

3. Understand your personal rights and boundaries.

4. Choose the pattern that you want to develop.

5. Practice new, positive habits that will form a framework for this new pattern.

Table 4.1

Good-Bye, Old Habits	*Hello, New Habits*
− Lack of boundaries	+ Boundaries in place
− Denying feelings	+ In touch with and expressing feelings appropriately
− Control; playing God; over-developed responsibility	+ Letting go; no more manipulation
− All-or-none	+ Balance; forget perfection
− Caretaking relationships with needy person	+ Equal, mature relationships
− Lack of trust	+ Gradual development of trust in self and others

6. **Surround yourself with supportive friends and professionals,** such as experts in domestic violence, counselors, lawyers, and doctors. Supportive friends and family can offer loving acceptance and help. Look to professionals for correct information, advocacy, and services appropriate to their field.

7. **Be patient and keep your eye on the BIG picture.** We all tend to get so caught up in the small details of our everyday lives that we lose sight of the broader view of what is happening. It is like being unable to see the forest for the trees. An example is when a woman is upset because her partner is angry that she is not making more money. He wants her to contribute more to the household expenses because he is spending most of his paycheck each week at the nearby casino. She apologizes and frantically looks for an additional job to please him, but she feels confused and irritated because she is tired and does not see how she can deal with another job or even where to start looking. When she tries to talk with him about how she feels, he gets abusive and will not talk. The reality is that she is being used and abused by this man and that he has total disregard for her well-being, her rights, and her dignity. Trying to make her way through the maze of living with him is a no-win situation. The

big picture here is recognizing her rights, facing the reality of her situation, and making specific plans to free herself safely from it. **Her life is ahead of her and full of wonderful possibilities.**

❏ **Stressing Positives**

- In Sessions I through III, you were presented with definitions and information on history. In this session, you are asked to take action for change in your lifelong habits. It is important to remember that it has taken years for you to get to this point and that the old habits will not disappear overnight. Be aware that your control and all-or-none issues make it hard for you to be patient with yourself in achieving gradual change. These types of changes are difficult for everyone. Keep in mind that you are taking in many new ideas that are working slowly like yeast in bread, and the process cannot be hurried. The more you love yourself, the faster it will proceed.

- You can choose how you want to live the rest of your life.

- Asking for help is a healthy sign—never a sign of weakness.

- Realistically cope with problems of rights and past unfairness. Pick your battles carefully and do not waste time on injustices over which you have no control. Focus on your goals and forget the rest.

- Compare yourself ONLY WITH YOURSELF. We all progress at different speeds and out of different situations. Only you can know when you are ready to make changes. Keep in mind how far you have already come.

- Do not be discouraged if you find practicing new habits uncomfortable and painful. It is like exercising unused muscles. Do it over and over and over again until the new habits feel comfortable and natural. BE CONTENT WITH BABY STEPS AND RELAX!

❏ **Assignment**

- Give yourself at least one gift this week.
- Study Session IV text and handouts.
- Choose your new patterns.
- Begin to practice your new habits.

❏ **Reference**

Gravitz, H. L., & Bowden, J. D. (1985). *Recovery: A guide for adult children of alcoholics*. New York: Simon & Schuster.

5

About Feelings: Grief, Fear, and Guilt

ALL FEELINGS ARE AS NATURAL AS BEING THIRSTY.
THERE IS NO RIGHT OR WRONG TO THEM. THEY JUST ARE!

❑ **Sadness and Grief**

When we talk about sadness and grief, we are talking about appropriate responses to loss of any kind. It may be loss of a loved one, of a relationship, of childhood, of a dream, of a sense of identity, or of a job or home. It may be because of a perceived failure. Whatever the cause, these feelings hurt badly, and we sometimes wonder whether it is normal to feel this way. Abused women particularly ask often what is the matter with them. To save themselves and their children, they have fled from an abusive situation in which they were terrified. So why are they now feeling so sad?

No matter how bad the abuse has been, when you leave a relationship into which you have poured your deepest commitment, your energy, your love, and all of your hopes, realize that this is a death. Do not be surprised if, all at

31

the same time, you feel relief from fear of the abuser but also terrible, heart-wrenching sadness. You may think it gets better for a few days, but you then may be struck again with the pain of loss. It often comes in waves, and each time you may think something is wrong with you because you do not seem to be making any progress. On the contrary, nothing is wrong with you except that you are grieving a serious loss; completing the process will take time. It is always like taking three steps up the mountain and then one step back. Keep in mind that you are on the way up to the top the entire time.

HOW TO MAKE IT GO AWAY

Step 1

Understand the stages of grieving and realize that every woman moves through them in her own order and at her own pace. The stages that most of us go through are **denial** ("I'm not sure I was really abused, and if I was, it wasn't all that bad."); **anger** ("He's not changing, and he won't change. It's not fair!"); **bargaining** ("Maybe I can get him to change if we have another baby."); **depression** ("I'm a failure. There's nothing to live for."); **acceptance** ("I did the best I could, and now I have to get on with my life. I know I'm a good person."); and finally **hope** ("I know now I have control over my own destiny.") (Kübler-Ross, 1969).

Step 2

Share your pain with caring persons who may be friends or professionals.

Step 3

Explore new possibilities for yourself, such as new doors to open, inner strengths to recognize for the first time and develop, and a new you with whom you now have the chance to become acquainted.

❏ **Fear and Anxiety**

Merriam-Webster's dictionary (1993) defines *fear* as "an unpleasant often strong emotion caused by anticipation or awareness of danger" (p. 425) and *anxiety* as "painful or apprehensive uneasiness of mind [usually] over an impending or anticipated ill . . . an abnormal and overwhelming sense of apprehension and fear often marked by physiological signs" (p. 53).

We all suffer from fear and anxiety at times, but for an abused woman trying to escape or to begin her life again without the abuser, these issues are a major concern. Panic attacks, during which a person may have heart palpitations, break out in a sweat, and be too terrified to move, are common. The first step in overcoming your fears is to identify them. Making a list of the things you are afraid of helps. It is important to recognize the difference between **realistic fear** ("My husband has threatened to kill me if I leave." "My child has a temperature of 105." "We're being evicted in a week.") and **chronic anxiety** ("I'm so scared all the time. I just never can pinpoint it, but I know something bad is going to happen."). Is what you are experiencing **a current, realistic, adult fear or anxiety, or is it an old terror** being reexperienced by you now? Is it **rational or irrational?**

WORKING OUT A RATIONAL FEAR

> I'm so scared of John. In the past, he's hit me and knocked me around, especially when he's been drinking, but nothing really serious. I guess I'm more scared now because he seems different. I don't know quite how. He just has a funny look in his eyes. I think he knows I'm getting ready to leave. I know he doesn't mean to hurt me. Underneath he's a really good person, and I still love him. He's the father of my kids, and they love him too. But I don't know what to do. I'm really confused and hardly know what's real anymore. Is it rational that I feel so scared and anxious all the time?

A woman who has been abused may often find it difficult to recognize whether her fears are realistic, particularly as they regard the abuse or the abuser. The abuser's verbal battering frequently leaves her unable to evaluate her perceptions. **The reality is that even if he has never laid a finger on you, it is rational to be afraid of your abuser.** Living with an abuser is living with a loose cannon. Abuse is usually an escalating process and rarely gets better. Its course is unpredictable and almost always becomes increasingly worse. It cannot be said too often that you are just as dead if you are pushed and hit your head the wrong way as you are if you are strangled! **If you are being abused in any way, be afraid!**

The priority in dealing with a rational fear is to be safe! Protecting yourself and your children may require your calling the police, leaving your home for a shelter or other safe place, and getting a temporary restraining order. **Always have an emergency safety plan in mind.**

Step 1

Gather information from knowledgeable persons about your options for taking action. Most important in this step is the term *knowledgeable person.* A knowledgeable person is one who specializes and has experience and training in the field. He or she has no personal investment in your decision making, has no axe to grind, and can look at the problem objectively. It is too easy, when you are upset, to listen to well-meaning friends and emotionally involved relatives, all of whom may have differing opinions on what you should do, when you should do it, and how. The end result is usually confusion and added stress. A more practical approach is to seek help, referrals, and information from knowledgeable persons, usually paid professionals in the field.

Step 2

Identify your choices.

Step 3

Make a decision about action that seems right to you.

Step 4

Be aware of your own powers.

Step 5

Be sure you are in a safe place for yourself and your children.

Step 6

Take action.

DEALING WITH AN IRRATIONAL FEAR

If you think your fears are irrational and probably related to previous terrors that are affecting you now, the best way to work them out is by talking with a counselor or therapist. An experienced person in that field can help you understand the source of your fears and teach you techniques for quieting them.

SOME TRUTHS ABOUT FEAR

Being afraid is part of being human. It is a feeling, shared with the animals, that we all have at times and that permits our species to survive. In addition to acute fears involving life and death matters, all of us experience fear or anxiety whenever we are in a new situation or approach the unknown. Doing something about it is the beginning of ridding yourself of the fear. The most painful fear of all is being afraid of being afraid, of panic attacks, and of feeling paralyzed, helpless, and depressed. It renders you unable to make decisions or take any action. You can begin to break this paralysis by realizing that **you do have choices and the power within you to take action. All you have to do is begin with one small step.**

❏ From Guilt to Responsibility

DEFINITIONS

Merriam-Webster's dictionary (1993) defines *guilt* as "feelings of culpability esp. for imagined offenses or from a sense of inadequacy" (p. 517). It is derived from Middle and Old English words meaning "delinquency." The derivation of the word *responsibility* is from Middle English and Latin words meaning "reply" (p. 998).

Guilt and self-blame focus all our attention on ourselves. The focus in responsibility is on communication with others, resolution of differences, and reconciliation. If you know objectively that you have done something hurtful to another person, it is appropriate to **accept responsibility**, apologize, make amends if possible, ask forgiveness, and then **let go of the guilt and move on.**

If, however, you are involved in a relationship with anyone, particularly a relative, and you sense that he or she is deriving satisfaction from controlling you and is trying to impose guilt trips on you when you have done nothing wrong, refuse to get hooked into the game. **If your sense of guilt comes from what you perceive as an inadequacy for never doing enough or being good enough, regard it as a guilt trip red flag.** A guilt trip conveys to the victim that you have done something terribly wrong or are inadequate. If you have become hooked into this, follow the steps back to reality.

STEPS TO REALITY

Step 1

Recognize the guilt trip as such. ("You are a bad mother because you've taken your children away from their father.")

Step 2

Analyze it. (Your priorities are for your children to be safe and to set for them a healthy example. They are not safe with an abusive father, even if he does not touch them.)

Step 3

Keep reminding yourself that you are not responsible or guilty. (The children's father chose to be abusive, and he alone is responsible for that choice.)

Step 4

Discipline your thinking, replacing negative thoughts with positive thoughts. The temptation to think negatively about yourself is always an assault on your identity. ("I am a good mother.")

Step 5

Distance yourself from the manipulator.

Step 6

LET GO. These are easy words but require hard work to achieve. Letting go means facing your inability to control others and recognizing each person's right to make and work through his or her own problems. It also demands acceptance of yourself and life as never being perfect. Some relationships and situations are not going to heal, and from these you must simply move on.

❏ **Stressing Positives**

- **Feelings are natural. Do not be surprised by or frightened of them.**

- **An old proverb says, "The truth will make you free, but first it will make you miserable." Do not be surprised when it temporarily does.**

- **What was overwhelming to you as a child need no longer overwhelm you now that you are an adult. You are no longer helpless; you now have the power to take action and control your own life.**

- **Panic attacks are terrifying, but people do not die from them.**

- **Learn not to run from, but rather to embrace, the pain. When you open your arms and accept your natural feelings of grief and fear, you also will be opening yourself to unexpected blessings.**

Table 5.1 Identifying Feelings

Feeling	Where I Felt It	Situation
Guilt	Knot in stomach	Ex-mother-in-law called

❏ Assignment

- Give a gift to yourself.
- Study Session V text and your handouts.
- Keep a chart this week on identifying feelings, as in Table 5.1.

❏ References

Kübler-Ross, E. (1969). *On death and dying.* New York: Macmillan.
Merriam-Webster, Inc. (1993). *Merriam-Webster's collegiate dictionary* (10th ed.). Springfield, MA: Author.

6

More About Feelings: Anger

❏ **Understanding Anger**

DEFINITION

Anger is one of the most difficult feelings for abused women to confront in themselves and, understandably, in others. Merriam-Webster's dictionary (1993) defines *anger* as "a strong feeling of displeasure and usually of antagonism" (p. 44). Synonyms are *rage, fury, indignation,* and *wrath.* **The feeling of anger is as natural as that of being thirsty.** Animals become angry when their territory is invaded. They become angry when their young, their herd, or they themselves are threatened. We humans become angry for the same natural reasons; it signals us that psychological or physical boundaries are being crossed against our wishes; our children, family, community, or selves are threatened with harm; needs are not met for human dignity, respect of rights, or justice; or we have become aware for the first time that any or all of the above have occurred in the past.

THE GIFT OF ANGER

Although it is easy to see the problems that may arise from anger that is inappropriately expressed, we must remember that anger also can be an exquisite gift. It has the wonderful capacity to move us into positive action against injustice and cruelty of all kinds. Most social progress has been born out of anger, and from it have come, for example, child labor laws to protect children from exploitation, the abolition of the slave trade, the vote for women, women's right to control their own bodies, social security, and laws protecting animals.

REASONS FOR BEING OUT OF TOUCH WITH ANGER

In looking at anger, it is important to remember that anger is neither good nor bad; **it just is!** Unfortunately, society places a heavy burden on women and their expression of anger: "Nice ladies are not supposed to get angry. They should be submissive, nurturing caretakers and peacemakers, with their men in charge. Only bitches show anger, and anger is sinful."

For the woman who has been a victim of abuse, particularly in childhood, anger in others can be particularly terrifying because, in past experience, it has always come to an aggressive, often violent conclusion. It is equally, if not more, threatening to begin looking at it in herself. In a severely dysfunctional childhood family, repression and denial of many feelings pervade the household and are often what permit an individual to survive. Children in that household spend their days frightened, walking on eggs, with their anger held rigidly in check. By adulthood, it has been under such total control for so long that the women are often unable to feel it at all. They are very fearful that if they allow themselves to be in touch with it, they will lose control totally and become violent. Anger is thought to be the same as violence; however, anger is energy and, if suppressed, will be turned inward and felt emotionally or physically. This inwardly turned anger is a primary cause of the extreme depression felt by so many abused women. Other typical responses are stomachaches, diarrhea, heart palpitations, shaking, crying, and emotional distancing.

❏ **Steps for Handling
the Anger Within Yourself**

Step 1

Recognize the feeling. A woman who has been out of touch with her anger may not be able to feel it for herself, but she may be able to be angry for her children or others. The "Anger Gauge" can help in identifying how it feels in regard to minor issues. Looking back at the "Abuse Index" section in Session

II text and the "How Serious Was Your Abuse" handout and identifying which rights have been violated may help trigger appropriate feelings of anger.

Step 2

Analyze the situation that is making you feel angry. Ask yourself: What am I really angry about? What is the actual problem? Whose problem is it? Do I really have power over this, or am I wasting my energy trying to control someone else?

Step 3

Release some of your internal anger energy. Remember that anger suppressed becomes like a volcano. You need to find ways to let it out gradually so that a gigantic eruption may be avoided. Sports, particularly running or walking, are excellent physical releases, as are exercises such as towel twisting, pounding on a pillow, using a punching bag, or screaming (though not at anyone). Try visualizing yourself doing something to release and be free of the anger. Keeping a journal or other written expression is a release that works well for many women.

Step 4

Surround yourself with supportive people and avoid others while you are working on this difficult issue. **Remember that anger and other feelings are issues that, in depth, should best be dealt with in counseling or therapy.**

❏ **Steps Toward Taking Action**

Step 1

Choose a goal specific to your anger-inducing situation and plan what you want to do.

Lisa's Situation

Lisa and Jake are in the process of a divorce, and he has been granted visitation every Saturday afternoon. When Jake comes to pick up the children at the house, he uses this as an excuse to see and harass Lisa. When their 5-year-old son answers the door for his dad, Jake pushes in, sits down in the living room, and takes his time about leaving. He looks through things on Lisa's desk, uses the bathroom, helps himself to food in the refrigerator, and has tried several times to corner her in the bedroom. Lisa is afraid it is only a matter of time until he tries to have sex with her. She has asked Jake not to come in, but he just laughs at her and tells her to lighten up. She feels scared, invaded, powerless, and very, very angry.

Lisa's Plan

Lisa is writing Jake a registered letter telling him that she no longer loves him, does not want to see or talk to him, and does not want him to come to the house. On Saturdays, she will drive the children to the public library (grocery store, police station, etc.) parking lot, where he may pick them up for visitation. She will meet them there again when it is time for the children to come home. A copy of the letter will be sent to both of their attorneys. She had never thought she would need a restraining order, but if this letter does not work, a TRO will be her next step.

Step 2

Understand what the block to action is. If something is preventing you from taking clear, vigorous action to confront the problem. It may be that the role of nonassertive, hurt, helpless victim, even though painful and frightening, is hard to get past because it is a familiar role. You know what to expect. In addition, even though your mind tells you otherwise, you may be reluctant to close the door to the abuser completely. You still may be hoping that if you love enough, forgive (see Session II), pray enough, and change yourself enough, you somehow will be able to make your abusive partner change. It is very scary to think about feeling anger and taking appropriate action. The next four sessions on Assertiveness Training focus on these issues and offer new ways of dealing with anger.

Step 3

Begin the action. If necessary, confront the person, agency, or whatever is the cause of the anger. If a continuing relationship is necessary or desirable, be assertive. If this is not what you want and if assertiveness is not working, do not be afraid to move from nonconfrontational assertiveness techniques into confrontation. **Use caution in this.** Keep in mind that your goal is to ensure that your rights are acknowledged and respected, but never deny the rights of others. **In abuse cases, your and your children's safety is primary.**

Step 4

Move vigorously toward your goal. Be a bulldog! Bulldogs, both male and female, are determined. Once they begin a course of action, they sink their teeth into whatever they are doing. They do not get discouraged or let go, no

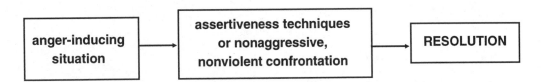

Figure 6.1. Anger Can Be Resolved

matter how big and powerful the opponent may be. Bulldogs hang on and refuse to be shaken loose. They let go when they are ready. In struggling through the legal system with abusers who usually hope that if they stall long enough and present enough complications the victim will give up in despair, women find that the bulldog philosophy is particularly applicable.

❏ **Stressing Positives**

- **Anger is a kind of energy. It can be a strong motivation for positive action and a sense of EMPOWERMENT.**

- **Anger is NOT a feeling to be feared. It is natural and can be channeled to your benefit. Let it work FOR YOU.**

- **Repressed anger is like a hard wedge stuck in one's side. When expressed appropriately, the wedge can come out and the wound can finally heal.**

- **The end result of anger need never be aggressiveness or violence. An anger-inducing situation may be approached with assertiveness techniques or nonaggressive, nonviolent confrontation. It can be resolved without any verbal or physical violence (see Figure 6.1).**

- **The best way to deal with anger is to seize control of your situation. When you no longer view yourself as a paralyzed captive, but rather as an empowered woman, the anger and need for revenge gradually will begin to recede. Finally, you will be able to let go of it all.**

- **After you have understood your rights, set your boundaries, and learned assertiveness techniques, you will be able to express your anger appropriately.**

❑ **Assignment**

- Give a gift to yourself.
- Study Session VI text and your handouts.
- Practice identifying when you are feeling angry and why, and take action to release your anger in a positive, appropriate way.

❑ **Reference**

Merriam-Webster, Inc. (1993). *Merriam-Webster's collegiate dictionary* (10th ed.). Springfield, MA: Author.

7

Boundary Setting Using Assertiveness Skills 1: Myth and Reality

❏ **What Is Assertiveness Skills Training?**

Assertiveness skills training teaches us how to set and enforce boundaries. These skills need to be taught or modeled and, once learned, can lead to a successful feeling of control and empowerment. The use of assertiveness skills helps reverse the cycle of abuse, frustration, and low self-esteem that occurs when one cannot claim rights or set boundaries (see Figure 7.1).

As we begin, it is essential to review "Your Bill of Rights" because assertiveness is the way to enforce them. These rights should belong to everyone, and assertiveness does not violate, but rather helps us respect the rights of others.

YOUR BILL OF RIGHTS

You have the right to be you.

You have the right to put yourself first.

You have the right to be safe.

You have the right to love and be loved.

You have the right to be treated with respect.

You have the right to be human—NOT PERFECT.

You have the right to be angry and protest if you are treated unfairly or abusively by anyone.

You have the right to your own privacy.

You have the right to your own opinions, to express them, and to be taken seriously.

You have the right to earn and control your own money.

You have the right to ask questions about anything that affects your life.

You have the right to make decisions that affect you.

You have the right to grow and change (and that includes changing your mind).

You have the right to say NO.

You have the right to make mistakes.

You have the right NOT to be responsible for other adults' problems.

You have the right not to be liked by everyone.

YOU HAVE THE RIGHT TO CONTROL YOUR OWN LIFE AND TO CHANGE IT IF YOU ARE NOT HAPPY WITH IT AS IT IS.

Figure 7.1. Nonassertiveness Circle

❏ Definition of Assertiveness

Assertiveness is the expressing of your own needs, wants, or feelings **without violating the rights of others.** When you are assertive, you are honest, direct, and sincere and treat other persons as equal and valuable. You also show respect for their rights, as well as your own. When you act assertively, you send the message that you are a worthwhile, confident person who knows her rights, recognizes her wants and needs, and is able to set boundaries. You feel empowered, proud, and in control, and your self-esteem will soar.

Using assertiveness skills does not guarantee that you will always get what you want. For battered women, using assertiveness with a batterer **may be very dangerous.** It is essential to assess your risk when attempting to set boundaries with an abusive person, especially a violent one. When used in a situation judged to be safe, however, such as with a nonabusive landlord, boss, attorney, relative, or friend, assertiveness will make you feel competent and powerful and that **you are choosing and controlling the directions in your life.**

As you move forward through Pattern Changing, you may have begun to realize that your abusive partner is not the only person in your life who treats you in an abusive manner. As you understand and define your boundaries, you may be surprised and alarmed to recognize that other people—people you never would have suspected in the past—are using or abusing you. Perhaps a boss, another relative, or someone you thought was a friend will come into focus as a person who is not really happy to see you change, who is criticizing you, belittling your efforts to grow, or ignoring your changes. It is with these people you will need to use your new assertiveness skills. In fact, most often it is with these people, and not with your abuser, that you will be setting limits. Keep this in mind as you experience assertiveness training.

❑ **Comparison of Assertive, Nonassertive, and Aggressive Behaviors**

One way to understand more clearly the definition of assertive behavior is to compare it with nonassertive and aggressive behaviors, the reasons for the behaviors, and the likely results of each (see Tables 7.1, 7.2, and 7.3).

❑ **Women and Assertiveness**

In our culture, women often are treated as "second-class citizens." This is a fact of life—one we must acknowledge and then move on. It is always important to pick your battles, and we are in this program to change what we have control over and can change—ourselves. It is helpful, though, to look at how our culture socializes women because it explains a lot about our own behavior. It is no small wonder that so many of us find it difficult to learn to be assertive when we have been socialized to be quiet, good, "seen and not heard," to "keep the peace," "not rock the boat," "turn the other cheek," or say nothing if we feel transgressed. That was expected of us as little girls and was rewarded by the adults in our lives. In other words, we were taught to be nonassertive. We were praised for being nonassertive, and we were punished for loud, confrontational, "boyish" behavior. We learned our lessons well. Now we must relearn them because if we remain nonassertive, we will never be able to protect the boundaries we have set or move forward toward change. We also must take into consideration our family backgrounds. For some of us who were raised in dysfunctional or abusive families, **nonassertiveness was essential in keeping us safe.** It was a highly effective survival technique. By becoming "invisible" in the family, one often was able to avoid verbal or physical attacks, criticism, punishment, or blame. As adults beginning to seek healthy changes and needing to distance ourselves from our

(Text continued on p. 52)

Table 7.1 Assertive Behaviors

Behavior	Reason	Result
You express your own needs, wants, or feelings **without violating the rights of others.** You are honest. You are sincere. You are direct.	To set boundaries. To gain direction. To achieve your goal to treat yourself as an equal, valuable person. To show you are worthwhile. To create honest, healthy relationships. To become empowered.	You gain respect and feel proud, powerful, worthwhile, sincere, self-directed, and in control of your own life.

EXAMPLE OF ASSERTIVE BEHAVIOR

Behavior	Reasons	Results
You are very upset because your attorney has not returned your many phone calls regarding a very important matter. You call his or her office, speak with the secretary, and say, "I'm very upset because my phone calls have not been returned. I need to make certain that my court date is not scheduled during the week I'm taking my children on vacation. I expect a call from him [or her] by 5:00 p.m. today."	(a) You want to be clear with your attorney that you are upset that he or she has not returned your many phone calls. (b) You want to be able to plan your vacation without having to worry about a court date conflict. (c) You want to give a time by which you need to be contacted to help give some structure to your attorney.	(a) Your attorney knows that you are upset. (b) Your attorney knows exactly why you are upset. (c) Your attorney knows what behavior you now expect. (d) You feel better about yourself because you have taken steps to get some control of an upsetting situation and have set some boundaries with an irresponsible attorney.

Table 7.2 Nonassertive Behavior

Behavior	Reason	Result
You do not express your own wants, needs, or ideas. You ignore your own rights. You allow others to take advantage of you. You don't say what or how you feel.	To avoid conflict or confrontation or possible injury. To be liked. Because you don't know any other way to be.	Anger; resentment; shame; frustration; powerlessness; feeling used, trapped, defeated, helpless, out of control.

EXAMPLE OF NONASSERTIVE BEHAVIOR

Behavior	Reasons	Results
You avoid calling your attorney. You call your attorney's secretary and leave the same message as in the past: "Please ask the attorney to call me." You complain about your attorney's irresponsible behavior to your family and friends. You constantly worry about the situation.	(a) You are concerned about offending your attorney. (b) You are afraid that if you are direct with your attorney, he or she may get angry with you. (c) You do not know how to tell your attorney that you are upset and why. (d) You believe that an attorney is an important person (and that you are not), and therefore it would not be appropriate for you to raise your concerns.	(a) Your attorney continues not to return your phone calls. (b) Your attorney never knows that you are upset and why. (c) You continue to pay for a service that you are not receiving. (d) You continue to worry about your vacation plans. (e) You feel bad about yourself because you are unable to deal with a situation that is upsetting you greatly.

Table 7.3 Aggressive Behavior

Behavior	Reason	Result
You express your feelings and needs **at the expense of others.** You violate the rights of others. You try to dominate.	You are angry, you want to achieve **your goal.** You don't want to deal with other persons' feelings. You don't know any other way to be.	Still feeling angry, guilty, and hungry for power and control. You are abusive to others and can be violent. You destroy relationships.

EXAMPLE OF AGGRESSIVE BEHAVIOR

Behavior	Reasons	Results
You call your attorney's secretary and scream at him or her because your "damn" attorney has not returned any of your phone calls.	(a) You do not know any other effective way to express your anger and frustration. (b) You have tolerated your attorney's irresponsible behavior for so long that you have just "had it." (c) In your family, when people are upset, they yell and scream.	(a) Your attorney labels you a "crazy, hysterical" woman and feels justified in not returning your calls. (b) You feel embarrassed and guilty because you "lost it" on the phone. (c) You have no resolution to your dilemma. (d) You feel bad about yourself and powerless because you have not been able to change this upsetting situation.

dysfunctional backgrounds, we now find that we are without the one skill that is essential for our growth: we have no knowledge of assertiveness and cannot claim our rights. We know only nonassertiveness and aggressiveness, and both leave us trapped in our present situation. Assertiveness may seem very scary. It can bring back memories of abuse. But **we are in the present, not the past. We are safe, and we can learn assertiveness techniques that will help keep us safe.** Remember that abusers probably will not be attracted to a woman who knows her rights, has set her boundaries, and is assertive. **Only by claiming our rights and setting and enforcing our boundaries are we able to move forward.**

Another important issue for women to consider is the fact that we place tremendous value on friendship, commitment, sensitivity, and loyalty. This is our gift as women. As battered women, however, we may find that we are extraordinarily committed and loyal, sometimes inappropriately so. When we begin to become assertive and set clear boundaries, we may have to risk losing some "friendships" that we have valued highly. We even may have to end loyalties that we discover are destructive to us. This would be difficult for any woman, but particularly so for us. We find it hard to quit and usually are determined to make relationships work. It is this very strength and determination, however, that we now can redirect toward learning assertiveness. It will help us define which friendships we should be valuing and which commitments we should honor. Risking the loss of friendships that you find destructive may seem frightening, but you need to ask yourself whether any so-called friendship or relationship based on one person's controlling another is worth saving. Finally, as women, it is well to be aware that our culture does not always initially respond positively to assertive women. Because our culture is male dominated, a woman with clear boundaries may be seen as a threat to the balance of power in the family or work environment. This can be negotiated, and common ground can be found. Some people who are unwilling to accept you may call you a "bitch." Prepare yourself to be called a "bitch" and know that the reality is far from the feeling that the label may give us. The reality is that **assertive boundary setting is done without violating another person's rights and therefore is healthy and considerate.** The "bitch" label arises because the other person is unhappy because he or she can no longer dominate or direct your decisions and because you are no longer the passive, nonassertive person he or she expects you to be. **If being a "bitch" means you are enforcing your boundaries, then be a bitch!**

❑ **Trusting Yourself to Be Assertive**

You can set boundaries, be assertive, claim your rights, and take control of your life. Trust yourself to try. Remember that it is okay not to be liked by everyone and that people will have more respect for you if you have boundaries. Many people have benefited from your nonassertiveness. They have used you to meet their own needs—at your expense. These people will be the first to criticize you for setting and enforcing boundaries. **That is okay. You do not need them.** You will be making new, healthy friendships in which you respect one another's life choices. Remember: Once you have learned assertiveness skills, you can choose if and when you want to use them. Your whole personality does not change; you simply now have a tool to use in directing your life.

❑ **Stumbling Blocks to Assertiveness**

In review, let's consider the eight stumbling blocks to learning assertiveness. Each has its valid concerns, but by examining, analyzing, and discussing them, we can identify how to conquer these pitfalls.

1. Cultural attitudes toward women

2. Fear of retaliation and conflict

3. Lack of knowledge of assertiveness as a skill

4. Fear of being labeled "a bitch"

5. Fear of losing friendships or other relationships

6. Fear of stirring up anger within oneself

7. Belief that we do not really deserve to be assertive (in control of our own lives)

8. Lack of readiness to assume responsibilities that may result from our being assertive

Trust yourself to try. You will be so proud that you did!

❏ **Some Myths About Assertiveness**

Since the concept of *assertiveness training* first came on the scene more than 20 years ago, it has spawned many myths. These myths have been generated by people who have no real understanding of what assertiveness really is. Unfortunately, these myths prevent people who really might benefit from acquiring assertiveness skills from learning them. Now that we have defined assertiveness and discussed its usefulness (and keeping in mind our Bill of Rights), let's look closely at some of these myths and understand why they are simply incorrect!

Myth: To be assertive, you have to be rude.

Reality: *Assertive skills* are based on showing respect for yourself and others. *Aggressiveness* is rude.

Myth: Assertive women are pushy women.

Reality: Assertive women have defined their needs and boundaries and can communicate them, showing respect, to others.

Myth: If you say no to a request, you are being selfish.

Reality: Saying no to a request is simply setting a boundary. Saying no can be done with thoughtfulness and consideration.

Myth: To be polite, you have to be nonassertive.

Reality: *Politeness* is courteousness. *Nonassertiveness* is the inability to communicate your needs and boundaries.

Myth: To ask someone for help is to show weakness.

Reality: To ask someone for help is to show that you know your *limitations,* as well as your *abilities.* Everyone needs help from time to time.

Myth: You have no right to question an important authority figure.

Reality: An authority figure may be an "important" person, but you have the same rights as he or she. You have the right to ask any question respectfully and to be given a satisfactory answer.

Myth: In our culture, only aggressive people are successful.

Reality: In our culture, aggressive people may seem to be successful, but often they are regarded with scorn and mistrust. Assertive people are respected.

Myth: Assertiveness means conflict, and you hate conflict.

Reality: *Aggressiveness* stirs up conflict. *Assertiveness* stirs up conflict only if you are dealing with a person who is unwilling to accept or respect your boundaries.

Myth: If you become assertive, people might stop liking you.

Reality: Healthy friendships grow with honesty and mutual respect. Assertiveness strengthens healthy relationships. An unhealthy friendship will wither under the demand for mutual respect. These "friends" are not true friends.

Myth: If you learn to use assertiveness, you might become a "bitch."

Reality: If you use assertive skills, which show respect for yourself and others, you will never be a "bitch." However, you may be called a bitch by anyone who is unwilling to acknowledge your legitimate needs and boundaries; that is their way of avoiding facing their own shortcomings.

❏ Assertiveness Practice

To have a successful first experience with speaking an assertive phrase, look into the mirror and practice saying the phrase, "I'm an intelligent, worthwhile person, and I value what I am learning in Pattern Changing." Remember that this is just a beginning, and you only have to say the words even though you may not believe them yet. This phrase would be an appropriate assertive response to anyone who questions why you attend those "crazy women's meetings" each week. **Good luck!**

❏ Stressing Positives

- **Remember that assertiveness is a skill that allows you to set and enforce your boundaries and to claim your rights. When you use assertiveness, you are honoring others' rights, as well as your own.**

- **By using assertiveness, you can help end the cycle of frustration and low self-esteem that occurs when you cannot set boundaries.**

- **Assertiveness is the KEY to successful pattern changing because it gives you the CONCRETE skill to apply your learning and to move forward.**

- **The nonassertiveness you learned as a childhood survival skill is NO LONGER HELPFUL IN YOUR LIFE TODAY. There were many good reasons why you became nonassertive, but now it is time to change.**

- **Trust yourself that you are worthwhile and that you deserve to set and protect your boundaries. You are ready to begin taking control of your future.**

- **Assertiveness = Boundaries = Control = Empowerment.**

❑ Assignment

- Give yourself at least one gift this week.

- Try to set a boundary *one time* this week.

- Identify a specific situation in your life that could be improved by using assertiveness. This might be a discussion with your attorney concerning his or her habit of not returning phone calls, or a request to your landlord to fix a broken front stair, or some other situation. At the next session, we will make note of these situations and use them as the basis for role-playing practice as we learn the basic assertiveness skills.

8

Boundary Setting Using Assertiveness Skills 2: Techniques

❑ **Rules for Assertiveness**

Your initial adventures into setting boundaries using assertiveness skills require *preparation and forethought.* When you are feeling uncomfortable or unhappy about a situation and you decide that you need to set a boundary, the following rules may be helpful. Specific techniques are explained in the next section.

1. Determine what your goals are. Exactly what do you want to accomplish or change?

2. Choose your wording carefully, use an "I" statement where appropriate, and be brief.

3. Practice your statement alone, in the mirror, or with a friend.

4. Address the situation as soon as possible. The longer you postpone setting a boundary, the harder the situation will be to change.

5. Prepare yourself that other persons may not like the fact that you are setting a boundary with them, and they may get nasty. If the exchange gets out of hand, *stop it.*

6. Avoid using the word *you,* as in, "I'm angry because *you* ignore my feelings." Stick to *I,* and talk about your own feelings and expectations, as in, "I'm angry when my feelings are ignored." *You* suggests blame and puts the other person on the defensive. *I* suggests that you are assuming what is your own responsibility.

7. Avoid pointing your finger at the other person. It is an aggressive gesture and also can put the other person on the defensive.

8. Avoid raising your voice. An assertive voice is just slightly louder than a normal conversational tone.

9. Avoid giving an ultimatum. Ultimatums are aggressive and usually result in the escalation of a problem situation.

10. If you are seated at the time of the encounter, sit slightly forward in your chair. This posture suggests confidence.

11. Keep constant eye contact, without staring or glaring. This shows confidence, poise, and purpose.

12. Have your facial expression agree with your message. If you are serious, look serious. Try not to smile or laugh if you are delivering serious news, no matter how nervous you may be.

13. **Stop yourself if you feel a need to apologize** for being assertive or raising a point. An apology implies that it is somehow improper to be setting a boundary, which is never the case.

14. **Repeat** your statement if necessary.

15. **Congratulate yourself for taking charge!**

❏ Assertiveness Techniques

The following three techniques—"I" messages, the broken record, and escaping from an encounter that gets out of control—allow you to (a) successfully choose the wording for your statements, (b) ensure that your words are heard and taken seriously, and (c) exit gracefully from a difficult situation. The rules for assertiveness, combined with these three techniques, will equip you to begin your adventure into boundary setting.

"I" MESSAGES

The first assertiveness technique is based loosely on the concept of "I" messages that is part of the popular Parent Effectiveness Training Program (Gordon, 1970). This technique may be used after you have identified an unsatisfactory situation and your goal is to change it. You would not use it for making or refusing a request, though you may choose it when confronting an authority figure or simply setting a boundary. These situations are covered in Session IX.

Assume that you are upset because a "friend" visits often and, coincidentally, brings her laundry and uses your washer/dryer and detergent. You realize that this friend appears only when she needs clean clothes. You have concluded that this person is using you. You have allowed the situation to continue, but now you want to set a boundary. An assertive statement that you might say to her is, "I feel upset when friends drop in, use my appliances, and then leave. I feel used. I'd rather meet somewhere for coffee and chat when there are no chores to worry about and we can just enjoy one another's company." In this statement, you have (a) identified your feelings ("I feel upset"); (b) described the situation in a nonblameful way ("when friends drop in, use my appliances, and then leave"); (c) explained the effect of the behavior on you ("I feel used"); and (d) described what behavior you would like to see instead ("I'd rather meet somewhere for coffee . . ."). This statement gives your friend a very clear message and a clearly defined boundary. If she is truly your friend, she will consider meeting you for coffee as you suggested.

This four-part sentence is very helpful in setting a boundary, but it does require some planning and practice. After you become accustomed to using the word *I*, labeling your feelings, explaining the effects of the behavior on you, and describing the behavior you would prefer, it will all seem easier and will become a habit.

BROKEN RECORD TECHNIQUE

The second assertiveness technique ensures that your words are heard and taken seriously. It is called the broken record technique. This is one of the most useful pieces of information that assertiveness training can teach you and is one of the most often used. It is effective when you are setting a boundary with someone and he or she is not hearing, not listening, or beginning to argue with you. It is a simple technique in which you make your assertive statement and, if necessary, repeat and repeat and repeat it.

The following is an example of a situation in which this technique would work well: You receive a phone call after dinner, and a man's voice greets you and begins describing a product he would like to sell you. You say simply, "No thank you. I'm not interested." He ignores your response and continues describing his product. You say, "No thank you, I'm really not interested." He asks you why, and you say, "I'm just not interested," and hang up. The tone of your voice should be slightly above your conversational tone, but do not speak angrily, just earnestly. This technique is very effective and requires much less effort than the "I" messages technique. This is reviewed again in Session IX, when we discuss dealing with authority figures.

ESCAPING FROM AN ENCOUNTER THAT GETS OUT OF CONTROL

The third assertiveness technique allows you to escape from an encounter when it seems to be getting out of control. This would include situations when the other person begins to get nasty, ridicules you, becomes sarcastic, insults you, makes an aggressive gesture, or begins a verbal barrage. You could say quickly, for instance, "This isn't working out the way I had hoped. Let's talk another time when things are calmer." Or you could say, "I have a right to be heard, and I have a right to be respected," or "I don't allow anyone to speak to me like that," and then turn and walk away or hang up the phone. Expect that the other person will be willing to work toward solving a problem and that he or she will avoid remarks that intend to hurt or demean you. If, however, the other person cannot respond in a civilized manner, end it. Remember that by responding inappropriately, the other person is attempting to retain power and control and to disregard your rights.

❏ **Stressing Positives**

- **This session covered a lot of how-to information about using assertiveness skills to set boundaries. It is very important to determine what your GOALS are when you approach an assertive encounter and to plan your STRATEGY with those goals in mind. A number of rules give you guidance on how to proceed, and they should be your ROAD MAP.**

- **The assertiveness techniques provide specifics about wording your sentences most effectively and prepare you to end quickly an encounter that has gotten out of control.**

- **Assertiveness training is another stepping stone on the road to change. It follows the steps of understanding the dynamics of abuse and of knowing your basic rights. We are building a highway to a new life.**

- **You have the right to be heard and to have your words and feelings respected. You deserve to be treated with respect.**

❏ **Assignment**

- Give yourself at least one gift this week.
- Continue to try to be assertive at least once this week.
- As in last week's assignment, be prepared to share a boundary-setting situation in your life that could be improved by using assertiveness skills.

❏ **Reference**

Gordon, T. (1970). *P.E.T.: Parent effectiveness training; the tested new way to raise responsible children.* New York: McKay.

9

Boundary Setting
Using Assertiveness Skills 3:
Requests and Authority Figures

❏ **Why Is Making a Request So Hard?**

IT IS HARD BECAUSE WE LACK SELF-WORTH.

Women in past Pattern Changing groups have told us that making a request is one of the most difficult assertiveness skills for them to practice. It is difficult for many reasons, but primarily because we tend to think we are not worthy enough to make a request of another person. Of course, we are worthy and need to treat ourselves as such. It is helpful to look again at "Your Bill of Rights" and remember that **you have the right to make any request. In so doing, you also assume the responsibility of accepting the other person's answer.**

IT IS HARD BECAUSE WE NEED TO BE IN CONTROL.

Perhaps another reason why making requests is hard is that we like to be in control, and we may view having to make a request as admitting the loss of control. As noted in previous sessions, most abused women have suffered from the unpredictable and chaotic nature of both their childhood and adult families, and they treasure the areas in which they are able to maintain some sense of control, be it real or imagined. Now, however, it is time to rethink the dynamics of control and requests. Viewed in the light of your new understanding of rights, boundaries, and assertiveness, making a request of anyone you wish is highly appropriate. Rather than indicate loss of control, it suggests you are a strong, capable woman with clear goals in mind, a woman unafraid to ask for appropriate assistance as you move toward these established goals. **Relax and trust yourself** as you learn to manage your resources wisely.

IT IS HARD BECAUSE WE FEAR REJECTION.

Still another reason why we avoid making a request is that when we do, we know we are opening the door for someone to say no. We already have endured our share of rejections, and risking another possible "no" is more than we can face. Unless you are dealing with an abusive person whom you already know, keep in mind that the other person is saying no to the *request*, and not to you *as a person*. It will be helpful if you can separate yourself from the request so that you will not feel personally rejected.

IT IS HARD BECAUSE WE THINK MAKING REQUESTS EQUALS USING SOMEONE.

A final reason why we hesitate to make requests is that we often have felt victimized by inappropriate requests made by users or abusers. We may equate making requests with using someone, and we do not want any part of that! The reality is that an assertive request is one that takes into consideration the other person's right to say no. Respect for that right and gracious acceptance of "no" builds trust in the relationship and lets both persons feel comfortable in making future requests.

SUGGESTIONS FOR MAKING REQUESTS

- Be specific. Give as much information as possible so that the person can make an informed decision. For example, "Could you help me distribute Girl Scout cookies on Friday, April 2nd, from 9:00 to 11:00 A.M. at city hall?"

- Do not begin by apologizing for the request that you are about to make. Apologizing suggests that your behavior is somehow incorrect or rude, and it certainly is not. An apology also can lend a negative tone to the message you are giving. For example, avoid saying, "Hi, Sue. I'm so sorry to be calling about this, but I need some help setting up the auditorium for the play tomorrow night." Instead, try, "Hi, Sue. I'm calling to ask if you might be available to help me set up the auditorium for the play tomorrow night. You'd need to plan on being there from 6:00 to 8:00 P.M." If your friend responds negatively, you could say, "Well, thanks anyway for considering my request. Maybe another time." Then, perhaps you could chat for a short time to show you are accepting of her even though she was not able to help.

- Do not beat around the bush when you are making a request. After some very brief chatting, get right to the point. In this way, the other person is clear about the purpose of the conversation and will not feel manipulated. For instance, you could begin a phone conversation by saying, "Hi, Marilyn, this is Beth. How are you enjoying this beautiful weather? I'm calling because I need to ask you for some help in typing up the handouts for next Wednesday's class."

❏ **Why Is Refusing a Request So Hard?**

IT IS HARD BECAUSE WE HAVE NEVER
BEEN TAUGHT THE ASSERTIVE WAY TO SAY NO.

Refusing a request is another assertiveness skill that can give us difficulty. Our group members often ask, "Why do I always end up saying yes when I know I want to say no?" **Remember that you have the right to refuse any request.** Refusing a request is simply setting a boundary that you have decided to establish.

IT IS HARD BECAUSE IT SEEMS SELFISH.

Another reason why we have problems refusing a request is that we have been socialized to think it is selfish, especially for a woman, to refuse requests. After all, aren't women the ones who put others' needs before their own, and aren't we the ones whose job it is to make others happy? Not anymore! We certainly can do these things if we choose, but now we know we have other choices as well. Now you know that saying no is setting a realistic boundary around what works best for you and your family.

IT IS HARD BECAUSE WE
WANT TO BE LIKED BY EVERYONE.

Perhaps another reason why we cannot say no easily is that it means so much to us to be liked by everyone. So much of our identity is connected with pleasing others and meeting with their approval that we are reluctant to risk losing that approval by saying no. Remember that the "new you" is forming your own identity by considering yourself and setting boundaries that are healthy for you. A person who respects your rights will like you even if you say no.

IT IS HARD BECAUSE WE WANT
TO APPEAR TO HANDLE EVERYTHING.

Many of us have prided ourselves on being able to handle anything that comes our way. People praise us for shouldering many responsibilities, and we like that kind of praise. In truth, we really have endured too many burdens, and it is time for us to share these burdens with others. We do not need to prove our worth to other people or to ourselves anymore, especially by trying to take on more responsibility. It is okay to make requests. **You are a worthwhile person!**

IT IS HARD BECAUSE IT MIGHT BE DANGEROUS.

Finally, we do not feel comfortable saying no because we fear it could be dangerous and could result in violent consequences. When an abuser is involved, the fear may be realistic, but in other situations, it simply may be a carryover from past abusive experiences. **Safety should always be the priority.**

SUGGESTIONS FOR REFUSING A REQUEST

- **When you say no, say it clearly and without any detailed explanations.** A person accustomed to manipulating you will argue with all parts of your explanation. Remember that anyone who respects your rights will accept your answer without questioning you. For example, in response to a request to baby-sit a neighbor's children this evening, you could say, "I have other plans for tonight, and I'll be out all evening."

- (This suggestion is our favorite!) **You can postpone your decision!** If you are unsure about the request, or if you want to say no but do not have the courage, ask for time to think about it. For example, you could reply to the above baby-sitting request with, "Hmm, let me check my calendar and call you back in a few minutes." For other requests, you could postpone answering by saying, "I'd like to think about it and also check my schedule. Let me call you back tomorrow around noon." These kinds of responses allow you time to decide what you want to say and to muster your courage. But do call back when you say you will because, by doing so, you are showing respect for the other person's rights.

- Just as we suggested in "Making a Request," **minimize your apologies,** particularly when you are setting a limit with someone who has been using you. Sometimes, apologies are appropriate and considerate, but not when you are dealing with a user or an abuser. For example, a proper apology would be, "I'm sorry, I just won't be able to make the meeting tonight. I have another commitment."

- If you refuse a request, you can choose to **invite the person to ask you again,** but only if you really mean it. By inviting another request, you are sending the message that you like that person and value the relationship. For example, you could say, "I'm sorry I can't help you tonight, but please call me the next time. I'd like to be of some help to you."

❏ Dealing With Authority Figures

Dealing with authority figures is another challenging assertiveness skill. An authority figure is anyone whom you perceive as having power over you. For battered women, many people can be included in this category: a boss, parent, attorney, social worker, doctor, therapist, teacher, and, of course, your abuser. It is difficult to be assertive with these people for many reasons, but primarily because we put them on a pedestal and grant them special rights. **They have the same rights as you and should respect your rights.** They may have more knowledge or a higher position, but **everyone has the same rights!**

SUGGESTIONS FOR DEALING WITH AUTHORITY FIGURES

- Keep in mind the broken record technique. Authority figures may try to dismiss your comments or ignore your opinions, and that technique is a very effective way of getting their attention.

- If you sense that the authority figure is hostile or abusive, get away from him quickly. **Never stay in a situation where you sense danger!**

- Most authority figures, such as doctors and lawyers, are really quite human and respond well when they are treated as the equals they truly are. In fact, they even may feel relieved to be taken off of their pedestals.

Picture them in your mind as *just normal persons,* and you will not be as intimidated in asking questions or giving your opinion.

❏ **Stressing Positives**

- **This session has dealt with three of the most difficult areas for battered women using assertiveness skills to set boundaries: making a request, refusing a request, and dealing with authority figures. Remember that you are a worthy, capable woman, and you are setting your boundaries so that you can survive and change. You are making requests because you acknowledge that we all need help to grow; you are refusing requests because you are learning your limitations and what is best for yourself and your children.**

- **You are earning respect for setting these boundaries. You are moving ahead, and only those people who wish to see you fail will object to your new direction.**

❏ **Assignment**

- This week's assignment is the same as for Session VIII.

10

Boundary Setting Using Assertiveness Skills 4: Practice

❏ **Practicing Assertiveness Skills**

Try practicing an assertive phrase that sets a boundary with an authority figure. This can be a challenging task, but you will feel so much more in control of your life when you can do it! Review "Dealing With Authority Figures" (see Session IX) and "Assertiveness Techniques" (see Session VIII) before you begin.

Our example will concern your imaginary attorney who almost never returns your phone calls and, when he or she does, acts annoyed and as if he or she were doing you a favor. You have mentioned your concern about this to your attorney a few times, but nothing has changed. Your goals are (a) to let him or her know that you consider not returning your calls unprofessional behavior; (b) to ask him or her to return your phone calls within one or two business days; and (c) to explain that if the situation continues unchanged, you will have no choice but to dismiss him or her and hire another attorney.

Try saying, "I feel frustrated and angry that none of my phone calls are being returned promptly. I am also upset by the fact that when they are returned, I am made to feel like a nuisance or an annoyance. I consider this behavior unprofessional, and in the future, I expect my phone calls to be returned within one or two business days. I look forward to our resolution of this issue, but if we can't resolve it, I will have no choice but to hire another attorney." You may think this is a very strong statement, but remember that the attorney's behavior is highly unprofessional. He or she would not be acting this way if you were a large corporate client, and this behavior suggests that there may be other parts of your case that the attorney might be mishandling. We frequently hear of situations like this, and it is important that you act on it to ensure that your future is protected. **You can do it!**

❑ Assertiveness and Anger

Session VI involved considerable information and discussion about the subject of anger, and we find it helpful to reintroduce that subject at this point in the program. Past participants in Pattern Changing groups have told us that the process of learning to set boundaries and be assertive sometimes stirs up anger within them. For some, this anger can be upsetting, scary, or confusing, so it is helpful to discuss it again, especially within the context of assertiveness.

Remember that anger is a normal, healthy, human emotion that we all have. Unfortunately, it often has been accompanied by violence and abuse in your life and consequently may be difficult for you to identify and express. Anger is at different points of intensity at different times for all of us. When you accept that you have rights, can establish boundaries, and know how to use assertiveness techniques, you begin to feel empowered. With this new sense of empowerment, hidden angers often begin to emerge. They emerge as part of the awakening that comes with being able to successfully set and defend boundaries. When you feel some control, you may realize how violated your rights and boundaries really were and the extent to which you were taken advantage of and used. This realization can make you very, very mad. **It is healthy to feel this anger.** You should be angry at all that has been done to you. But now **you have the skill of assertiveness,** which allows you to express your appropriate anger successfully without fear of its ever becoming an uncontrolled explosion. You know how to use the techniques you learned in Session VIII to express it assertively and to rid yourself of the anger, to take control, and to channel your energy toward continuing positive changes in your life.

❑ A Word of Caution

When women first begin to practice assertiveness techniques, they sometimes go through a period of "feeling their oats" and trying it out on everyone around them. Sometimes, they think that if they become assertive enough, this will change their abuser's behavior. It is important to remember that his problem of abuse will not change unless he receives a great deal of professional help. His overtly abusive behavior may go underground briefly in response to your new assertiveness, but it probably will be expressed in subtler ways, such as "jumping the gun" on getting a restraining order, concealing assets, other legal shenanigans, or manipulating the children. **Use balance and common sense and wait patiently. Be careful!**

❑ **Stressing Positives**

- **Congratulations on completing these four sessions on boundary setting using assertiveness. It is not easy, and you have made wonderful progress.**

- **Setting boundaries is critical in choosing new directions in your life. Assertiveness is a skill for making your choices possible. You are moving ahead. You are empowered.**

- **As you move forward and feel confident enough to remember the past, do not be afraid of feeling your anger. You now know how to express it assertively, appropriately, and without hurting yourself or others.**

- **As you practice your new skills, never forget that SAFETY IS YOUR PRIORITY. BALANCE AND COMMON SENSE SHOULD BE YOUR GUIDES. If you are dealing with an abuser, be extremely cautious in displaying your new assertiveness. If you are likely to be involved in a court process, protect yourself and your children by consulting an attorney before making any major changes or decisions. NEVER "TIP YOUR HAND"**

❑ **Assignment**

- Give yourself at least one gift this week.
- Continue practicing assertiveness and setting boundaries.
- Next week we will be talking about our goals. Begin thinking about the following questions:

  – What kind of person would you like to be in 6 months?
    In 5 years?

– What kind of work would you like to be doing in 6 months? In 5 years?

– Where would you like to be living in 6 months? In 5 years?

11

Setting Realistic Goals

❏ **How to Set Realistic Goals**

The prerequisite for arriving at realistic goals is to be in touch with your feelings, your values, and your dreams—not your parents', not your partner's, but *yours!* Understanding where your interests and talents lie and assessing how much energy you have form a common sense platform for asking some basic questions. If you could be any kind of person, anywhere, doing anything you choose, what kind of person would you be? What kind of work would you do? Where would you live? These are dream goals, and, although it is important to be realistic in facing barriers to them, remember that dreams can lead you to reality when you are willing to use them as jumping-off places. Viewing goal setting in that way and being flexible and willing to compromise permit you to plot out your own realistic, achievable goals. Remember that your goals, particularly long-range goals, are not carved in stone and may be changed when and how you wish.

❏ **Achieving Your Goals**

Recognizing that you have set your goals carefully and realistically makes achieving them much simpler. Goal setting for you and your abuser was rarely successful as you frantically sought to make things better by getting him into counseling or AA, stopping him from going out with his buddies every night, moving farther away from his abusive family, and so forth. Your failed goals, then, always were focused on keeping peace and making him happy so that your dreams could begin to come true. Today, you no longer build your goals on denial and fantasy but can anticipate succeeding because you now realistically base them on yourself. A positive attitude of expectancy of progress smooths the achievement process and hastens your ultimate success.

BEGIN TO DO IT

Make a plan by writing down your short- and long-range goals; under each put the steps you think will be necessary in order to achieve them. Set small daily goals for yourself to begin to accomplish each step; then proceed to complete them. Check them off as they are done. If an approach does not seem to be working, assess it objectively and do not be afraid to make changes. You have been clear and vigorous in setting your goals, and now you are doing your best in an orderly way to accomplish them. Keeping in mind the common tendency of expecting perfection of oneself, approach the project with flexibility, patience, and acceptance of yourself as simply human.

SUPPORT DURING THE PROCESS

This is an exciting time as you move toward your goals. It requires commitment, determination, and lots of energy. It is a time for surrounding yourself with caring, supportive persons and for avoiding nonsupportive relatives and friends. A supportive person puts energy into your life and does not drain yours. He or she also has no vested interest in keeping you dependent.

Working toward your goals is also a particularly appropriate time for asking knowledgeable persons for help. Depending on your goals, legal advocates, educators, and social service agencies may have valuable information and services that are exactly what you need at this moment. Do not be afraid to ask; then be open to receive whatever they can offer that is helpful.

THE ROLE OF COUNSELING

It is appropriate to seek counseling when you are going through a crisis, such as being in or leaving an abusive relationship; grieving a death or serious illness in the family; feeling depressed, isolated, and panicked; and wanting to be in better touch with what you are feeling, why you are feeling it, and how to express those feelings in positive ways. We often forget that counseling is a particularly helpful resource at a time when you are moving in new directions, developing new habits and patterns, and expending considerable energy.

Many people fear counseling because they are afraid of what they will find out. Sometimes they fear opening a door that might unleash monsters inside themselves. Often they think that going to a counselor means they are crazy. This feeling is particularly threatening for abused or formerly abused women because they were taunted often by their abusers as being "sick, crazy, needing mental help, or needing to be locked up." They also fear what other people will think.

The reality about counseling is that it does not mean a person is crazy, nor does it imply weakness or lack of independence. You do not consider yourself weak if you wear glasses to improve vision or if you ask a surgeon to set your broken leg so that you will be able to walk. Counseling is a highly practical and empowering option in helping you better understand yourself and work through changes, crises, or long-term problems. Do not be afraid of the word *problems*. Having problems is part of being alive, and everyone has them. Finding ways to solve them is part of the adventure.

CHOOSING A COUNSELOR

Counseling is an adventure of mapping uncharted territory in oneself. It is the light going on in the dark closet so that you can finally see clearly your scary childhood monsters and recognize your adult power over them. It is not a threatening outsider trying to get inside your head to control you. It is, rather, a supportive outsider helping you get inside your own head to understand yourself better. Precisely because the counselor is an objective outsider, he or she can see what you are too close to the problem to recognize.

If you decide to seek counseling, ask a knowledgeable person for referrals and remember that you have the right to shop around. It is appropriate to mention that you are doing so when you call for an appointment. Tell the secretary that you are interested in meeting the counselor to see whether he or she may be the right person for you and ask about a fee for the initial visit. Decide whether you want a woman or a man and do not make a decision on the spot if you do not think this person is just right for you. It is of primary importance that you feel comfortable with whomever you choose. You may want to ask the prospective counselor some of the following questions:

- When abuse is the issue, do you believe in couple counseling? Be the abuse physical or emotional, it is our experience that couple counseling is never helpful and can, indeed, be dangerous if physical abuse is involved. At that point, the woman can never feel safe in being totally honest with the counselor if her abuser is there with her. If she tells the truth, she may well return home with him to be beaten or verbally battered; if she cannot be honest with the counselor, there is little purpose in being there. Only in later stages of the abuser's changing is it appropriate even to think of couple counseling. In our opinion, the abuser needs education, behavior modification, and individual counseling for at least a year before it is safe for the victim to accompany him for help. A counselor who does not understand this has had little experience in working with abuse.

- Have you had much experience with battered women? With incest survivors? With survivors of other childhood abuse?

- What are your fees?

- How often do you want to be paid?

- Which insurance coverage do you accept?

- What will happen if it runs out?

- Will you charge me if I call in sick?

- How long do you think my counseling will require?

❏ **I Need . . . , I Want . . . , I Deserve . . .**

In thinking about goals, you may feel reluctant to focus on goals just for you. It can be a helpful exercise to practice saying, "I need . . . , I want . . . , (and particularly) I deserve . . ." Women who have been abused tend to feel guilty when they say it, just as many of you did in the beginning when you thought about giving yourself gifts. Now, giving gifts comes more easily, and practicing "I deserve . . ." will make you more receptive to and accepting of your own worthiness.

❏ **Stressing Positives**

- **Listen to and trust yourself and your own feelings. This is the beginning of finding out who you really are.**
- **You deserve goals that will make you feel happy and complete, and you deserve to succeed in achieving them.**

- Take good care of yourself with health care, diet, exercise, and appearance. YOU DESERVE IT!

- Let yourself begin to experience being the child you never had the chance to be. HAVE FUN! Life is meant to be enjoyed, not just endured and survived.

- Be patient with your progress. Do not be discouraged when life seems like two steps forward and one step back. It is that way for everyone. Keep your eye on the big picture of where you are going and how far you have gone already.

- Develop a sense of humor and REMEMBER TO BE A BULLDOG!

❑ **Assignment**

- Give a gift to yourself.
- Study Session XI text and handouts.
- Practice saying, "I need . . . , I want . . . , and I deserve . . ."
- Next week, we shall talk about decision making. Be thinking about any difficult decision making you would like to share with the group for support and help.

12

New Patterns
of Decision Making

❑ Why Decision Making Is So Difficult

Decision making, not unlike goal setting, can strike a note of fear in women who have been abused. You may believe that many of your past decisions have been wrong, ill-conceived, and the cause of pain, fear, and unhappiness. They may have left you too paralyzed to face even small decisions and with little faith that you will not continue repeating the same mistakes. The old need to be perfect and in total control keeps you terrified of making "wrong" decisions, and equating a decision that did not work out with total failure makes trying again highly risky.

❑ Decision Making in a New Light

The first step in decision making is to change the focus from the abuse situation and the wishes of others to the short- and long-term goals you have defined for yourself. Emphasis should be on your own inner growth and on knowing that with each decision you make, you are increasing your understanding of yourself, your growth toward completeness in yourself, and your self-empowerment. Most significant of all is an emerging realization that true security lies in recognizing your own ability to handle whatever presents itself in your life. When you view yourself in this way, you cannot fail, no matter what choice you make. You will have gained new insights, had new experiences, and have no need to repeat the same mistakes.

In past decision making as an abused woman, your focus usually has been on goals external to yourself. You have had to make such decisions as whether to remortgage your house to help him buy a new boat so that he will love you more; whether you should move away so that his old drinking buddies will not be around to influence him; whether you should give up your job because he hates your working outside your home; whether, for the sake of your children, you should put up with a man who regularly beats you, and whether you should let your chronically alcoholic parent come live with you because she is your mother.

Perhaps most complicated is deciding whether to remain with an abuser who is not currently dangerous physically, is getting help, and is beginning to show changes, but whom you no longer love and want to leave. What holds you there is that you cannot support yourself and your children, and no decent and affordable housing is available. Abused women in this situation frequently make the decision to stay for the time being. They may feel guilty because they feel they are compromising their feelings and new understanding for material considerations, and they worry about what others will think. Know that no one's situation is exactly like that of another, and **only you can know what is right for you at this moment.** Responses to the most difficult decisions are often not clearly all right or all wrong, so careful weighing and compromise must be involved. Whatever your decision, you have the right to be respected and accepted by others. If this is your situation and you have decided to remain with or return to your abuser, an important factor, in addition to physical safety, is your emotional well-being. You will need considerable support from outside your home to sustain your sense of rights and boundaries for yourself and your children.

❏ Decision-Making Steps

1. Define the problem and set your goal.

2. Ask for expert advice.

3. List alternatives.

4. Look at the consequences of each.

5. Weigh the pros and cons of each.

6. *Make a decision based on reason, not emotion, balancing your negativism and unrealistic romanticism with objectivity.*

❑ **After the Decision**

Researchers working to find a cure for a disease will conceive of a possible new approach, examine it in the light of previously done research, decide to pursue it, and may, after years and much data collection, realize that their hypothesis simply has not worked out as conceived. The researchers will be disappointed, but they will not consider the effort to have been a worthless failure. From the process much has been learned that can be applied elsewhere. No one will need to repeat this work in seeking a cure for that specific disease, and occasionally, the results are found to be useful in attacking a different disease.

In the same way, once you make your decision, it is important to assume total responsibility for it. Evaluate the results, and if it is not working out well, make changes as they seem appropriate. **Remember that you have the right to make a mistake, recognize it, and change your mind.** List for yourself what you have learned from the decision and then **let go of it and move on.**

❑ **Stressing Positives**

- **Most abused women find, after looking back over their lives, that their decisions that brought them the most pain were based entirely on emotion, never on reason. ALL BIG DECISIONS AND MANY SMALL ONES SHOULD BE BASED ON REASON, NOT ON EMOTION. If feelings are to be weighed in decision making, let them come at the end of the process.**

- **It is not safe to return to an abuser, particularly if the abuse was physical or sexual, until he accepts responsibility for it, is seriously committed to changing himself, and has followed through for a year with counseling and education about HIS abuse problem. It has taken him years to become the way he is. His problem behavior will not disappear in a few weeks or months. BE CAREFUL!**

- **IF YOU HAVE CHILDREN, YOUR PRIORITY IN DECISION MAKING MUST BE THEIR WELL-BEING AND SAFETY. That is the parent's job even though, at a given point in their lives, they may not like your decisions.**

- **We constantly are changing and growing as individuals. Decisions are not forever and need never be carved in stone. Do not be afraid, after careful reasoning, to change your mind. It is okay.**

- **Success is daring to try. The only failure is not learning from our mistakes.**

❏ Assignment

- Remember to give gifts to yourself.
- Study Session XII text and handouts.

13

Healthy Relationships

❏ Do Healthy Relationships Really Exist?

It is understandably hard for a woman who has been abused, perhaps all her life, and who may never have experienced a healthy relationship to imagine what it is like or believe it can even exist. If you dream that a healthy relationship is one that arrives full-blown in the form of a perfect knight on a white horse who catapults you into a Brady Bunch existence, you would be quite right in not believing that such a relationship exists. Reality teaches us that this scenario rarely, if ever, occurs except in soap operas and sitcoms. Perfection in relationships, as in other areas of life, does not exist. A relationship grows gradually in health and strength because two people commit themselves to it and both work very hard and patiently to achieve a give-and-take balance. It requires a willingness for each to give not 50%, but 100%. It is impossible to have a healthy relationship with an abuser who will not admit his problems or seek extensive professional help for them.

❏ How Healthy Relationships Begin

Persons who like themselves, believe they have rights, and have their boundaries in place tend to be attracted to and attract healthy relationships.

81

Healthy relationships may begin in ways that seem similar to unhealthy ones. Two people may be attracted to one another because of mutual interests and "chemistry" and feel the high of being in love. Feeling this way in the beginning of a love relationship is natural and exciting, but it is not realistic to imagine that this intensity can be sustained for long. A mature, healthy relationship grows slowly and patiently beyond that, with both partners willing to give commitment, thought, and work to building a deep sharing of life together. Romance is kept alive by growing love, thoughtfulness, and hard work by both partners. All relationships, healthy and unhealthy, vary in duration, intimacy, and balance. They do not stand still, but rather are constantly evolving.

❏ How a Healthy Relationship Feels

In a healthy relationship, partners are equal and neither is in a position of control. They are best friends. They trust and depend on one another and are not in competition, so the need to keep up one's guard does not exist. They are willing to listen to one another and try to communicate honestly and clearly, never assuming that the other is a mind reader. Each is willing to acknowledge shortcomings and work on them and is not afraid to say, "I'm sorry." Each partner makes the other feel his or her best—supported, accepted, appreciated, and loved. **It is an extra dividend if the partners have a sense of humor!**

❏ Problems, Conflicts, and Disagreements

All relationships, no matter how healthy, have problems, conflicts, and disagreements. Sometimes the partners get angry and may yell, but working disagreements through together, using fairness and assertiveness (see Table 13.1), challenges couples to strengthen and grow and is a natural part of being a family. The style one uses in disagreements or fights is an important factor that differentiates the healthy from the unhealthy. The goal is to grow individually and as a couple.

Table 13.1 Fairness and Unfairness in Disagreements

Fair	Unfair
+ No fear of violence or verbal abuse.	− The threat of abuse is always present.
+ The current issue of disagreement is discussed.	− The current issue gets clouded by bringing up past problems, blaming relatives, etc.
+ Honest communication of feelings by using assertiveness techniques.	− Denial of facts and attempts to put partner on the defensive.
+ Speaking one at a time.	− Constant interruptions, ignoring, or refusing to talk.
+ Agreed-on time out when tensions rise.	− Tensions escalate to explosion point.
+ Respect.	− Personal insults, name calling.
+ Willingness to say, "I'm sorry."	− Refusal to admit when wrong and tendency to blame others.
+ Both win by growing in understanding in the relationship.	**− The person in control wins over the other.**

❑ We All Need a Sense of Family

In the midst of unavoidable stresses in today's world, we all suffer from pressures of external events such as death, loss of job, and moving. We also must come face-to-face with the pain of life's deepest terrors and struggles—ultimate aloneness, fear of death, the meaning of life, and the search for our identity. The presence of mature, healing companions—be they an intimate partner, other family members, or close friends—supports, strengthens, and encourages us as we confront these challenges.

As they emerge from abusive situations, most women find it a meaningless exercise to consider aspects of healthy relationships as achievable realities. These women usually are feeling confused and guilty, are grieving, and are in no mood to look at what might be considered daydreaming nonsense. Stinnett and De Frain (1985) have done considerable research on strong families, and we believe their observations can provide guidance and encouragement to women whose sense of family has been destroyed.

QUALITIES THAT STRONG FAMILIES SHARE

Commitment. Members of strong families are dedicated to promoting each other's welfare and happiness. They value the unity of the family.

Appreciation. Members of strong families show great appreciation for each other.

Communication. Members of strong families have good communication skills and spend a lot of time talking with each other.

Time. Strong families spend time—quality time in large quantities—with each other.

Spiritual Wellness. Whether they go to formal religious services or not, strong-family members have a sense of a greater good or power in life, and that belief gives them strength and purpose.

Coping Ability. Members of strong families view stress or crises as an opportunity to grow.

These six qualities allow members of strong families to interact, connect, and reinforce each other to form a net of strength all around them.

❑ **Making the Strengths of Strong Families a Part of Your Life**

If you are a woman alone, a single parent, or burdened with nonsupportive, destructive parents and siblings, you may feel discouraged and may believe that the qualities of the strong families just described are unachievable for you. It is true that at this moment your family is not intact, but if you study the qualities one by one you may discover that at least some of them, despite your situation, are already present in your life in relationships with your children, friends in the group, or coworkers. If they are present, you have an opportunity, with your new awareness, to work on strengthening them. If they do not exist for you now, you can explore ways to develop them through new contacts, groups, volunteer work, church, and so forth.

❑ **Stressing Positives**

- **Evaluate the strong-family qualities already present in your life and explore ways to fill the gaps.**

- **Remember that the key to healthy relationships is to love yourself.**

- **Loving yourself requires an understanding of your rights, an ability to set boundaries, and some mastery of assertiveness techniques.**

❑ **Assignment**

- Remember gifts for yourself.
- Study Session XIII text and handout.
- Spend some time thinking about progress you think you have made since beginning Pattern Changing. If you have been keeping a journal, it is helpful to review it.

❑ **Reference**

Stinnett, N., & De Frain, J. (1985). *Secrets of strong families.* New York: Berkley.

14

Changed Patterns

☐ **New Understanding**

When one arrives at this point in Pattern Changing, it is interesting to look again at the "Pattern Changing Outcome Goals for Participants" from Session I. If you have kept a journal during the program, it too will help you recognize your progress. "Your Bill of Rights" is becoming a daily guideline in defining values and making reasoned decisions. You understand the abuse problem and family dynamics that are involved and are particularly aware of the fact that abuse is about control and is 100% the abuser's problem. You no longer think you are responsible for it in any way, and you know that no one deserves to be abused. You are well aware that when physical or sexual abuse is involved in a relationship, this is not just a "We all have problems, nobody's perfect" situation, as abusers and victims in denial often say. It is criminal, prosecutable behavior and should never be confused with the normal ups and downs of a healthy relationship. The only difference between physical and emotional abuse is that you cannot prosecute the latter. However, it hurts at least as much and is as damaging to both the victim and her children.

An important aspect of your new understanding is that you see reality much more clearly and, when you have questions, you are aware of how to proceed. You are not afraid to ask knowledgeable persons for information and feedback, and you know that many answers can be found through reading. You can sift through your information until you feel good about your sense of direction. Another vital piece in your new understanding is that you are better able to recognize the differences between love, infatuation, and addiction, and you have an awareness of what to avoid. You know the "red flags" in men's behavior that signal danger in a relationship: little or no respect for your rights and boundaries; abusiveness; controlling behavior; a need for mothering; overprotectiveness of you; jealousy; possessiveness; willingness to let you pick up more than your share of expenses, or pressure to combine all of your assets with his; reluctance to assume responsibility for his own mistakes; a tendency to blame others; an inability to say, "I'm sorry"; and addictions and/or dysfunctional childhood legacies for which he has been unwilling to get counseling.

❏ Practiced Techniques Form New Patterns

As you patiently and with baby steps have practiced your chosen habits, you can see how they have begun to create a framework for new patterns. You are aware of your basic rights and are beginning to define your boundaries. Assertiveness techniques are becoming more comfortable for you. Your new goals are realistic ones, not created out of fantasy or wishful thinking, and you try to base important decisions on reason, not emotion. When being with another person makes you feel uncomfortable, frightened, ashamed, or not good about yourself, you now appropriately distance yourself from that person. You also can achieve appropriate distance from people and situations which at one time you felt you had to control. You are not afraid now to reach out to friends and ask for support, nor are you too timid to request information from appropriate sources. You now see the grays, as well as the blacks and whites, and feel much more balanced in your view of life. You are more comfortable with talking, feeling, and trusting, more in touch with your inner self, and able now to say, "I need, I want, I deserve."

❏ Stressing Positives

- **Closure is sad for all of us, but it is also very exciting. When one door closes, another opens to new experiences, new opportunities, and new possibilities.**

- **As a woman empowered by awareness of her rights and with her boundaries in place, you are no longer vulnerable to needy, controlling relationships.**

- You can practice letting go of the old identity of being an abuse victim. It is a thing of the past, and now you can move on.

- The temptation is always present to step back into the habits of the past. Remember that one step back and two steps forward are to be expected. Do not be angry at yourself when you step back, but dare to wait expectantly for a sense of direction from within yourself to take the next steps forward.

- Confront, don't avoid, temptation. Know yourself and recognize that the temptation of old habits is always an assault on your real identity.

- The path to freedom from the past is motivation, forgiveness and LOVE OF YOURSELF, clearly defined goals, decisions made, actions taken, and EMPOWERMENT.

- Joy is an inner sense not dependent on others. Real security is trusting yourself to handle any situation.

❑ **Assignment**

- Remember to give a gift to yourself.
- Study Session XIV and your handouts.
- Cook/provide for the potluck supper next week.
- Choose something precious to you that you want to share with the group—for example, a favorite quotation, something you have written yourself, a talent you have, a skill you can demonstrate. Next week will be your choice to "show and tell" with the group.

APPENDIX
Forms, Handouts,
and Questionnaires

1. PATTERN CHANGING GROUND RULES

The Pattern Changing Program is designed to help a woman understand the problem of domestic abuse that has been a pattern in her life, recognize her power and choices, and learn techniques for achieving her goals. **Pattern Changing is education, not therapy, and cannot solve crises.**

1. **CONFIDENTIALITY** is primary. Because all women attending will be sharing personal information, it is a basic rule that no one disclose to anyone outside the group what is said or the identity of anyone in the group. *Suspected child abuse is the only exception to the confidentiality rule, as we are mandated by law to report it to the Department of Children, Youth and Families.*

2. **CONSISTENT ATTENDANCE.** Pattern Changing always has a waiting list, so we ask that you be seriously committed to attending all 15 sessions. Call the office if you have to be absent for any reason.

3. **PROMPTNESS.** Out of respect for the other women, be on time, as latecomers are disruptive. If you have a problem arriving on time because of your work or other schedule, speak with the leaders about it. **We begin promptly** at 6:30 p.m.

4. Particularly in the beginning sessions, many women find some of the information **DEPRESSING OR UPSETTING.** This is understandable because the subject matter may revive old issues. If this happens to you, do not just stop coming. Speak with one of the leaders immediately, and she will offer you help in moving through these rough and discouraging spots and will support you in deciding what you want to do. You are not alone in these feelings, but most women find that if they stick with it, the pain lessens and is replaced by positive understanding of one's own power and capacities.

5. **SENSITIVITY TO OTHERS.** We have only 2 hours for each session. Every woman needs her chance to be heard, and it is important to be sensitive to this. No one should monopolize the discussion.

6. If you are having a **PROBLEM WITH ANOTHER WOMAN OR SITUATION IN THE GROUP,** consult the coleaders after the session.

7. **NOTE TAKING** is discouraged, because it may interfere with feeling connected to the other women in the group. *It is not necessary because the text is handed out at the end of each session.*

8. If **TRANSPORTATION** is a problem, mention it in the group and try to arrange a car pool with other participants.

9. Do not drink **ALCOHOL** or use **OTHER DRUGS** prior to coming to the group. Pattern Changing is an educational program, and a clear head is needed. In addition, because of past experiences with alcoholics, many of the women are uncomfortable with the odor of alcohol.

10. **SMOKING** is not permitted in our building. A break may be arranged if you feel the need for it.

2. PATTERN CHANGING REGISTRATION FORM

DATE _____ DATE OF BIRTH _____

NAME _____

ADDRESS _____

_____

HOME PHONE _____

NAME OF EMPLOYER _____

WORK PHONE _____

PERSON TO BE CALLED IN EMERGENCY _____

_____

PHONE NUMBER _____

_____

3. CONTRACT FOR
PATTERN CHANGING PARTICIPANTS

The Pattern Changing Program is presented twice a year, in the fall and spring, with group enrollment limited to 15 women. Because Pattern Changing always has a waiting list, we ask that participants make a commitment to on-time attendance at the 15 sessions. Fees for attending are on a sliding scale from $30.00 to $1.00 each session. The registration fee is $15.00.

Confidentiality is a particularly serious issue in the Pattern Changing groups. Group leaders, other staff, volunteers, and child care workers have signed confidentiality statements, and we ask that participants do so too. Breach of confidentiality will result in immediate expulsion from the group.

STATEMENT OF COMMITMENT
AND CONFIDENTIALITY

I agree to attend all 15 sessions of Pattern Changing and to be prompt. If I have a good reason for not attending or for arriving late, I shall notify the leaders.

I understand the importance of confidentiality in the Pattern Changing Program. I promise never to disclose to anyone outside the group the identity of or information about the other participants.

I agree to pay a fee of $ _____ per session for the Pattern Changing Program, to be paid weekly.

Signature _____

Witness_____

Date_____

4. PATTERN CHANGING PROGRAM
CONFIDENTIAL INFORMATION

Date _____

Marital Status

      _____Married   _____Widowed

      _____Separated   _____Single

      _____Divorced   _____Living With Partner

Number of Children _____

Ages of Children _____

Legal Involvement (Check all that apply)

      _____Have TRO (temporary restraining order)

      _____In process of divorce

      _____Seeking child custody

      _____Seeking support

      _____Charges being pressed against partner for sexual abuse
            of my child(ren)

      _____Is a government agency involved?

            If so, name of caseworker_____

      _____Do you have legal representation?

            If so, name of attorney or legal assistant_____

Religious Affiliation _____

Individual Counseling

      _____Currently   Name of counselor:_____

      _____Previously   Name of counselor:_____

HISTORY

Adult

Current alcohol abuse ....Y N   In recovery.......Y N

Current other drug abuse.....................................Y N   In recovery.......Y N

Ever medicated for emotional problems............Y N

Ever hospitalized for emotional problems.........Y N

Ever attempted suicide ....Y N

Physical abuse ....Y N

Emotional abuse..Y N

Sexual abuse ....Y N

Number of abusive adult relationships _____

Number of alcoholic or other drug-addicted partners _____

Childhood

Physical abuse ....Y N

Emotional abuse..Y N

Sexual abuse ....Y N

    If yes, was the abuser a relative (incest)? .....Y N

Physical abuse of other children in family.........Y N

Sexual abuse of other children in family............Y N

Adults were abusive to one another ....Y N

Adults abused alcohol or other drugs................Y N

NAME _____

DATE OF BIRTH_____

5. PATTERN CHANGING
PROGRESS QUESTIONNAIRE

1. **Emotional abuse is just as abusive as physical abuse.**   true____ false____

2. An abusive person usually cannot help what he or she does.   true____ false____

3. Love and tenderness can change an abusive man or woman into a good partner.   true____ false____

4. I am often not sure whether my partner's behavior is really abusive.   true____false____

5. I feel that somehow I am to blame for the abuse I have had.   true____false ____

6. I have to forgive my abuser even if he never says he is sorry.   true____ false____

7. I have to stay with my abusive partner because he is a wonderful dad, and children need a father.   true____ false____

8. It is selfish to ever put myself first.   true____ false____

9. I do not know how to say no to other people.   true____ false____

10. It is bad to get angry.   true____ false____

11. I am not sure what my rights really are.   true____ false____

12. I do not know how to ask for what I know is rightfully mine.   true____ false____

13. Other people often seem to have more control over my life than I do.   true____ false____

14. Sometimes I feel as if my problems are different from those of anybody else.   true____ false ____

15. I often feel depressed and do not have much hope for the future.   true____ false ____

NAME_____ DATE _____

6. YOUR BILL OF RIGHTS

- You have the right to be you.

- You have the right to put yourself first.

- You have the right to be safe.

- You have the right to love and be loved.

- You have the right to be treated with respect.

- You have the right to be human—NOT PERFECT.

- You have the right to be angry and protest if you are treated unfairly or abusively by anyone.

- You have the right to your own privacy.

- You have the right to your own opinions, to express them, and to be taken seriously.

- You have the right to earn and control your own money.

- You have the right to ask questions about anything that affects your life.

- You have the right to make decisions that affect you.

- You have the right to grow and change (and that includes changing your mind).

- You have the right to say NO.

- You have the right to make mistakes.

- You have the right NOT to be responsible for other adults' problems.

- You have the right not to be liked by everyone.

- **YOU HAVE THE RIGHT TO CONTROL YOUR OWN LIFE AND TO CHANGE IT IF YOU ARE NOT HAPPY WITH IT AS IT IS.**

7. OUTCOME GOALS FOR PATTERN CHANGING PARTICIPANTS

1. **To increase understanding of**

   a. basic rights

   b. abuse

   c. abusive family dynamics

   d. dysfunctional family legacies

   e. feelings, with emphasis on anger, fear and anxiety, guilt, and grief

   f. healthy relationships

2. **To gather information about and learn techniques for developing**

   a. boundary setting

   b. assertiveness

   c. realistic goal setting

   d. decision making

3. **To receive support and encouragement**

   a. while growing in self-knowledge and self-esteem

   b. in recognizing and digesting painful, as well as freeing, realities

   c. in struggling to develop the above techniques

   d. **in changing negative lifelong patterns to positive patterns of your own choosing as an adult woman**

8. HOW SERIOUS WAS YOUR ABUSE?

Circle the response that best describes your current or past relationship.

1. Does he check up on you and want to know where you are at all times?

Often	Sometimes	Rarely	Never
3	2	1	0

2. Is he jealous, and does he accuse you of having affairs with other men or women?

Often	Sometimes	Rarely	Never
3	2	1	0

3. Does he tell you you are stupid, lazy, ugly, a rotten cook, a failure as a wife or mother, or no good in bed, etc.?

Often	Sometimes	Rarely	Never
3	2	1	0

4. Does he call you obscene names?

Often	Sometimes	Rarely	Never
3	2	1	0

5. Does he tell you that no one else could ever love you?

Often	Sometimes	Rarely	Never
3	2	1	0

6. Does he make fun of you in front of other people?

Often	Sometimes	Rarely	Never
3	2	1	0

7. Does he try to keep you from seeing family or friends?

Often	Sometimes	Rarely	Never
3	2	1	0

8. Does he control the family money so that you have to account for every penny and/or beg him for it?

Often	Sometimes	Rarely	Never
3	2	1	0

9. Does he forbid or demand that you work, or, if you want to work, does he make it difficult for you?

Often	Sometimes	Rarely	Never
3	2	1	0

10. Does he tell you that no one would ever hire you?

Often	Sometimes	Rarely	Never
3	2	1	0

11. Does he try to keep you from driving the car by taking your keys or a part of the engine?

Often	Sometimes	Rarely	Never
3	2	1	0

12. Does he have dramatic mood swings?

Often	Sometimes	Rarely	Never
3	2	1	0

13. Does he become angrier when he drinks?

Often	Sometimes	Rarely	Never
3	2	1	0

14. Does he try to make you have sex when you don't want to?

Often	Sometimes	Rarely	Never
3	2	1	0

15. Does he force or pressure you to commit sexual acts that you are not comfortable with or consider unnatural?

Often	Sometimes	Rarely	Never
3	2	1	0

16. Has he ever broken or damaged your home, possessions, or property, or dumped garbage in your home?

Often	Sometimes	Rarely	Never
6	5	4	0

17. Has he ever hurt or killed a pet in order to frighten or punish you?

Often	Sometimes	Rarely	Never
6	5	4	0

18. Does he ever lock you in a room or out of the house?

Often	Sometimes	Rarely	Never
6	5	4	0

19. Does he ever push you, shove you against walls, or restrain you by holding you to prevent you from leaving a room?

Often	Sometimes	Rarely	Never
6	5	4	0

20. Does he ever force you to stay awake?

Often	Sometimes	Rarely	Never
6	5	4	0

21. Does he ever slap, punch, kick, bite, choke, pull your hair, or burn you?

Often	Sometimes	Rarely	Never
6	5	4	0

22. Does he ever hurt you with an object or weapon (gun, knife, cigarette, rope, belt, etc.)?

Often	Sometimes	Rarely	Never
6	5	4	0

23. Has he ever threatened you with an object or weapon?

Often	Sometimes	Rarely	Never
6	5	4	0

24. Does he endanger you or your children by reckless driving?

Often	Sometimes	Rarely	Never
6	5	4	0

25. Does he neglect you or the children when you are sick or in need of medical help?

Often	Sometimes	Rarely	Never
6	5	4	0

26. Has he ever threatened to kill himself, you, your children, or other family members or friends?

Often	Sometimes	Rarely	Never
6	5	4	0

27. Has he ever been violent toward your children?

Often	Sometimes	Rarely	Never
6	5	4	0

28. Has he ever molested your children sexually or behaved toward them in an inappropriate, flirtatious way?

Often	Sometimes	Rarely	Never
6	5	4	0

29. Is he ever violent to other people outside the family?

Often	Sometimes	Rarely	Never
6	5	4	0

30. Have you ever had to call the police, or wanted to, because you feared him?

Often	Sometimes	Rarely	Never
6	5	4	0

31. Has he ever been arrested for violence?

Yes	No
6	0

32. When he senses that you cannot stand the abusive behavior any longer and are thinking about leaving, does he try to manipulate you to stay by making you feel guilty, threatening suicide, etc.?

Often	Sometimes	Rarely	Never
3	2	1	0

To learn how serious your abuse has been, total your circled points.

0–14	Nonabusive
15–36	Moderately abusive
37–93	Seriously abusive
94 or more	DANGEROUSLY ABUSIVE

Note: This abuse index is based on the CSR Abuse Index, in A. Shupe and W. Stacey, *The family secret*, pp. 221-222. Copyright © 1983 by Anson Shupe and William Stacey. Used with permission.

9. ANGER GAUGE

The purpose of this gauge is to help you recognize that you can be angry about minor things, identify the feeling, and begin to feel less threatened by it. In each situation described below, indicate by writing *yes* or *no* whether you felt at all angry.

1. _____ You are already late for work and find that your car has a flat tire.
2. _____ You have worked all summer planting vegetables and flowers, and you discover one morning that neighborhood dogs have trampled the entire garden.
3. _____ Your roof has been leaking after a storm, and you call a repairman to fix it. He promises to arrive the next day but never shows up and doesn't call.
4. _____ You call him again, assuming there may have been miscommunication. Another date is made, but again he doesn't show up or call.
5. _____ You have been waiting to be served at the deli counter for 10 minutes. Just as your turn comes, another person pushes ahead of you.
6. _____ When you give the checker in the grocery store your canvas bag to use instead of paper or plastic, she ignores it and begins loading your groceries into a plastic bag.
7. _____ When you call this to her attention, she is unpleasant and acts annoyed.
8. _____ You lend someone a book, and he or she does not return it.
9. _____ You repeatedly make plans to go to dinner with a friend, and she is always a half hour late.
10. _____ You are in a hurry to get to an appointment, but the car in front of you is traveling below the speed limit and will not speed up.
11. _____ You are trying to discuss your feelings about a relationship issue with someone you love, but the other person clams up and will not talk.
12. _____ You are chatting with two other people at a meeting. A third person join the group and greets the other two but ignores you.
13. _____ You send in an insurance claim, and the company tries not to pay.
14. _____ You have bought expensive tickets for a concert, but when you get there, you find that you are seated almost behind a pillar.
15. _____ A coworker never has a good word of appreciation or encouragement to say about your efforts.
16. _____ A friend lies to you over a minor issue.
17. _____ You have had to wait an hour and a half for your doctor's appointment even though you called ahead and were told he was on time.
18. _____ You have been waiting for a car to leave a crowded parking lot so that you can park in its space. Just as it leaves, another driver who has just arrived races in ahead of you.
19. _____ Your brand new car is having serious engine trouble.
20. _____ You spill indelible ink on your new dress.

---

10. EVALUATING RELATIONSHIPS: HEALTHY OR UNHEALTHY?

Susan and Larry

Susan is an independent, quick-to-make-decisions kind of person. She has an exciting career as a marine biologist and makes an excellent salary. Larry has never been to college but is very happy in his career as a cabinet maker. He does beautiful work and is much in demand. He is a quiet man, contemplative and kind. His shop is in their home, so he often is more available to their three children, all in elementary school, than is Susan. Sometimes Susan feels impatient with him because he does not make decisions as quickly as she does. Susan's impatience hurts Larry's feelings now and then. At those times, he tells her how he feels, and Susan remembers to slow down. Susan had two alcoholic parents but has had many years in Adult Children of Alcoholics (ACOA), as well as individual therapy, and tries to be aware of the negative patterns in her life. Susan and Larry share a deep commitment to their church, where they met, and are enthusiastic hikers and campers with their children.

Elizabeth and Joe

Elizabeth and her husband, Joe, are having a terrible financial struggle. They are heavily in debt and have four children to raise, all of whom are in school. Elizabeth wants to take a job, both to help with finances and because she is eager to have a career in addition to her homemaking. Joe will not hear of it. "No wife of mine is going to work! I want you at home." She is always home when her children get home from school.

Jenny

Jenny is a single working mother. She cannot always be home when Johnny, her 8-year-old son, gets home from school, so she has arranged with Mrs. Jones, an elderly widow next door, to keep Johnny until she gets home. Jenny is sometimes an hour or so late. Johnny knows exactly what to do when he arrives home and Jenny is not there. He likes Mrs. Jones. Jenny's mother and father think she and Johnny should move in with them so that someone will always be there for Johnny, but Jenny wants to keep her own place and independence. Sometimes, though, it is a financial struggle for her, and she wonders whether she is being fair to Johnny.

Ellen and Ralph

Ellen and Ralph have been together for a year and are still madly in love. She is a schoolteacher, and he is a football coach in the same school. He does not feel ready to get married, and neither of them is interested in having children in the near future, if ever. They fight a lot because Ralph is very jealous of Ellen and would like her to be less independent and more tuned in to him. His passion is sports, and they spend much of their free time going to games. He likes Ellen to watch when their school's basketball team plays or when the football team he coaches plays. Ellen loves to please him because he treats her "like a queen."

Paloma

Paloma is a single mother with four children under 10. Her ex-husband was a severe abuser, and she is afraid of emotional involvement with another man. She is very committed to her children. Recently, she met Jorge at the restaurant where she cooks, and he has been calling her often. He says he is especially attracted to her marvelous qualities as a mother and the fact that she puts her children first. He says his mother was terribly abusive to him and his father when he was a child, and he wishes she had been like Paloma. Paloma has gone out with Jorge a few times, and it has been a pleasant time—movies, dinner, and so on. Jorge has never been married and does not talk about marriage at this point.

Roger and Louise

Roger is a fisherman; he is away for many days at a time. He is an alcoholic but has been in recovery for 6 years, thanks to AA and individual counseling. The fishing industry is not doing well these days, and he worries about the future. Louise comes from a farming community in Minnesota. She and Roger met while she was in Rhode Island visiting her sister. They have been married for 5 years and have 3-year-old twin boys. Roger does not want his wife to work, and Louise loves staying home with her children, just as her mother did when she was growing up. She has a small at-home business growing flowers and vegetables for several restaurants and is proud to see her own bank account growing. When Roger is home, they enjoy seeing their families and going square dancing.

Jane and Alex

Jane is a single mother with four children under 10. Her ex-husband was a severe abuser, and she is afraid of emotional involvement with another man. She is very committed to her children. She is on welfare and plans to go to school, if possible, when her baby starts kindergarten in a year. Alex lives next door. He is divorced from a woman he says was neurotic and impossible to live with. He loves to come by Jane's for dinner because he thinks her cooking is the best he has ever eaten. He is part owner of a bowling alley and likes his work. Jane is very lonely for adult companionship, and he is good company. They laugh a lot. He can never take her out, even though he always says he wants to, because she cannot afford to hire a baby-sitter. Lately, after the children are asleep, she has made love with him, but she is frightened because she is finding herself waiting more and more eagerly for his phone call or the sound of his footsteps at the door. She has told him she wants to get married again, and he has not said no.

Rashida and Jamil

Both Rashida and Jamil are in real estate and are hard-driving business persons. They are quite competitive and fight a lot, rather explosively, though never abusively, usually about minor things around the house. Once the anger is out, they both cool down immediately and kiss and make up. They love to go to the dog races with their circle of friends. They party a lot, though neither of them drinks much. They plan to buy a house and think they will get married eventually. They are not sure they want to have children because they both enjoy their work and independence.

Julia and Norman

Julia met Norman when he was a patient for minor surgery in the hospital where she works as an R.N. She is the supervisor of nurses on her floor and loves her job. She is very successful at it and feels well respected by her colleagues. Julia has never been married and has always been timid about involvements with men because she was sexually abused by her grandfather when she was a small child. She has had some therapy for this but knows she eventually will need more help. Norman had a small construction business that was thriving until the recession. They dated for 6 months, and he was extremely sensitive and thoughtful to her. She told him about her childhood, and he was very understanding. They got married, and he moved into Julia's house. Unfortunately, the recession has almost ruined Norman's business, and he is just barely hanging on. Julia has mortgaged her house to help keep his business going. Norman has hurt his back and now is collecting temporary disability. Julia works very hard at her job and is trying to take good care of Norman. His mother was a tyrant, and his first wife cheated on him and cleaned out his bank account when she finally took off, and Julia hates to see him so miserable now. He spends his time watching television and playing cards with a few friends because he is not well enough to do any work. He is very depressed.

11. RECOMMENDED READING FOR PARTICIPANTS

Bass, Ellen and Davis, Laura. *The Courage to Heal.*

Dyer, Wayne. *Your Erroneous Zones.*

Engel, Beverly. *The Emotionally Abused Woman.*

Evans, Patricia. *The Verbally Abusive Relationship.*

Fracchia, Charles. *How to Be Single Creatively.*

Frankel, Lois. *Women, Anger, and Depression.*

Gravitz, Herbert L. and Bowden, Julie D. *Recovery: A Guide for Adult Children of Alcoholics.*

Humer, Judith Lewis. *Trauma and Recovery.*

Jeffers, Susan. *Feel the Fear and Do It Anyway.*

Jordan, Judith; Kaplan, Alexandra; Miller, Jean Baker; and Surrey, Janet. *Women's Growth in Connection.*

Krantzler, Mel. *Creative Divorce—A New Opportunity for Personal Growth.*

Ledray, Linda. *Recovering From Rape.*

Lerner, Harriet Goldhur. *Dance of Anger.*

Lerner, Harriet Goldhur. *Dance of Intimacy.*

Martin, Del. *Battered Wives.*

McNulty, Faith. *The Burning Bed.*

Nicarthy, Ginny. *Getting Free: A Handbook for Women in Abusive Relationships.*

Norwood, Robin. *Women Who Love Too Much.*

Pizzey, Erin. *Scream Quietly or the Neighbors Will Hear You.*

Priere, Lynette and Peacock, Richard. *Learning to Leave.*

Robertson, John. *Suddenly Single—Learning to Start Over.*

Schaeffer, Brenda. *Is It Love or Is It Addiction?*

Schaeffer, Brenda. *Signs of Healthy Love.*

Stearns, Ann Kaiser. *Surviving Personal Crisis.*

Stinnett, Nick and De Frain, John. *Secrets of Strong Families.*

Straus, Murray A., Gelles, Richard J., and Steinmetz, Suzanne. *Behind Closed Doors.*

Walker, Lenore. *The Battered Woman.*

---

12. PATTERN CHANGING PROGRAM EVALUATION

Date _____

1. The following topics were covered during Pattern Changing. Indicate how you felt about the amount of information given for each subject.

	Wanted more	Right amount	Wanted less
Physical abuse	_____	_____	_____
Emotional abuse	_____	_____	_____
Sexual abuse	_____	_____	_____
Why it is so hard to leave	_____	_____	_____
Dysfunctional family legacies	_____	_____	_____
Bill of Rights	_____	_____	_____
Understanding of personal boundaries	_____	_____	_____
Assertiveness	_____	_____	_____
Awareness of feelings	_____	_____	_____
Goal setting	_____	_____	_____
Decision making	_____	_____	_____
Healthy relationships	_____	_____	_____
Self-empowerment	_____	_____	_____

2. Would you like to see other topics discussed? Yes_____ No_____
   If yes, what other topics?

3. If it applied, was the idea of addiction to a person a helpful concept for you in seeing your way out of your own problems?

   Yes_____ No_____

   Please explain.

4. Was the Myers-Briggs information helpful?   Yes_____ No_____

   Why or why not?

	Very	Moderately	Not at all
5. Were the coleaders:			
sensitive to your needs?	_____	_____	_____
positive in their attitudes?	_____	_____	_____
knowledgeable about the subject?	_____	_____	_____
approachable?	_____	_____	_____

6. In what ways has the Pattern Changing Program affected your life?
   Do you do some things differently now? Give some examples of these
   changes.

7. What did you not enjoy about Pattern Changing and would like to see
   changed?

8. Do you have any other comments or concerns about the Pattern
   Changing Program?

CERTIFICATE OF
COMPLETION OF PATTERN CHANGING

_____

Extends congratulations to

_____

for completion of

THE PATTERN CHANGING PROGRAM

_____
Date

_____
Agency Director

_____
Pattern Changing Leader

_____
Pattern Changing Leader